Resounding Body

*Building Christlike Church
Communities through Music*

— ANDY THOMAS —

Sacristy
Press

Sacristy Press
PO Box 612, Durham, DH1 9HT

www.sacristy.co.uk

First published in 2020 by Sacristy Press, Durham

Sacristy Limited, registered in England & Wales, number 7565667

British Library Cataloguing-in-Publication Data
A catalogue record for the book is available from the British Library

ISBN 978-1-78959-112-5

"This is an insightful and very readable guide to music in worship, for churches where musical resources are thin. It will be helpful for any musician or minister wanting to develop their music in church. It roots music in a theology of inclusion and charts an encouraging way forward."

— **Giles Goddard**, *Vicar of St John's in Waterloo*

—

"This book will be an inspiration to all who are called to serve a congregation as church music leaders in a local parish situation. Full of hope and thoughtful ideas, it deals sensitively with many of the practical issues involved in including a wide range of people in the musical ministry. Highly recommended!"

— **Miles Quick**, *Head of Congregational & Instrumental Music, Royal School of Church Music*

—

"Had I possessed this book through my ministry, I would have been better pastorally enabled to work with musicians, singers and congregations, to meet their needs, and with them better to form the Body of Christ in the contexts in which I have served."

— **Andrew Pratt**, *Honorary Research Fellow, Luther King House, Manchester*

"Written in an engaging style, full of human stories and underpinned with solid theology, this book sets before us a vision of what church music and church musicians can be: signs and foretastes of the kingdom of God, learning in microcosm the lessons of being the body of Christ that the whole church needs to take on board. It is the perfect guide for any church that wants to focus on what really matters when setting up a choir or music group, and will provide refreshing food for thought, prayer and action for existing groups of church musicians."

— **Mark Earey**, *Director of Anglican Formation and Tutor in Liturgy and Worship, The Queen's Foundation for Ecumenical Theological Education*

—

"This book is a wonderful gift and encouragement! The author interweaves stories from his many years of experience as church organist and musical director with theological reflections on singing and music-making as part of the body of Christ. Used to working with small and under-confident groups of singers, he helps us to see how all can contribute to enrich the worship of the people of God. The COVID-19 pandemic, with its restrictions on corporate singing, has made us all the more aware how much music is an integral part of our worship, and this book gives hope and confidence for the times when we can sing again!"

— **Jan Berry**, *Honorary Research Fellow, Luther King House, Manchester*

For Dad

Contents

Acknowledgements

Thank you, Giles Goddard, Shanon Shah, Elisabeth Sutcliffe, Adrian Alker and Ian McIntosh who offered useful comments on drafts of the book. Thank you, Natalie Watson, for your patience, invaluable guidance and insightful comments. Thank you, dearest Roz, for supporting me throughout, reading several drafts and sending me back to the drawing board on a number of points. Above all, thank you to the unforgettable choir of St John's, Waterloo, and to the various worshiping communities with whom I have worked over the years.

Introduction

St John's is a middle-of-the-road Anglican church. Its tall spire rises above a building that, if it wasn't for the spire, could be mistaken for a Greek temple, with its six-column portico and rectangular design. The church is situated in a busy part of town near a very busy train station. Crowds of people pass it on their way to and from work every day.

St John's ticks over with a typical attendance at its main Sunday service of around eighty. Most are retired or nearing retirement with a sprinkling of young families. The church crypt—a rather shabby space that is accessible by stairs only—is home to a number of businesses and charities. The rental income from these, other church bookings and a modest level of giving by the congregation, keeps the books balanced year by year.

The musical accompaniment for the main Sunday service consists of a long-standing organist and a hymn book. The organist is competent and loyal, but only interested in playing the organ. A limited range of hymns and other sung bits are used every Sunday. The congregational singing is invariably weak and a little reluctant.

That is the way the music at St John's has been for many years. There is the occasional conversation after church that laments the lack of a regular choir or instrumental group—something to make the musical scene feel *alive*—but overall, the congregation seems to accept the way things are. The vicar, who is relatively new and busy with other priorities, is also resigned to the status quo for the time being. There is no one to drive forward any real change.

—

Many worshipping communities, of all denominations across the UK and beyond, have few musical resources. There may be a small choir or instrumental group, led by a determined but frustrated volunteer who faces dwindling numbers and other limitations on what they can do. Increasingly, there may only be an organist or pianist, or perhaps just recorded music, and a sense that there is no potential to develop anything more.

This is how I found St John's, Waterloo, London when I arrived in October 2010. I had recently moved to London to take a job in the civil service and left behind a musical director role in a church in Sheffield. I had found a community choir to conduct in the meantime, but it wasn't the same as leading music in church. A good friend recommended St John's, and so

I went along with my (then) girlfriend to check it out. We felt at ease and intrigued by a community that was hugely diverse, yet deeply inclusive. Several different nationalities; LGBTQ+ and straight; the theologically liberal and conservative: all existed alongside each other in apparent harmony. Canon Giles Goddard, the vicar, clearly had ambitions. It felt like an exciting place to be.

Soon after I arrived, Giles and I met. We found that my approach worked alongside his vision for St John's, so we agreed that I would attempt to develop the music on a voluntary basis. My primary task would be to build a choir, drawing people from the congregation.

What followed was a learning experience that I shall never forget, and that inspired me to reflect in more detail on the purpose of church music. This book is the product of those reflections.

Its purpose is a rallying cry to all music leaders in situations like St John's, where musical resources are limited and expectations are low. My aim is to persuade those who are grappling with a small choir or instrumental group to persevere; and to convince those who are tempted by the idea of developing something in their community to step up—perhaps by leading a few singers or instrumentalists, or teaching the congregation some short songs or rounds.

The reason we should step up and keep going is because we are doing something fundamentally important. We are helping to build what St Paul referred to as the "body of Christ": to transform individuals and communities to be more Christlike. This transformation process does not require faultless, high-end music; yet, as musicians, we naturally focus (or are judged by others) on how the music is sounding and forget the equally important and fundamental reason we are doing what we do. Consequently, we quickly get frustrated and give up when it isn't sounding good. The aim here is to correct this imbalance.

Another symptom of focusing too much on the notes and not enough on the community is a temptation to rest on our laurels when the choir or instrumental group is sounding great, rather than working to ensure that the rest of the congregation has an opportunity to offer their voice or instrument in worship. Consequently, the second purpose of this book is to challenge music leaders, in all contexts, who do not focus enough on building the body of Christ, and consequently miss opportunities to transform and invigorate their communities.

Drawing on recent scholarship and twenty-five years' experience of leading music in church, I suggest how building and maintaining a choir in low-resource contexts contributes to this transformative process. How it enables the choir members and the gathered community to engage more closely with the Spirit which, for Paul, is the fundamental force that knits the body together. How it encourages those who are part of the worshipping community to act in a more loving and inclusive way towards one another, and towards those beyond the church. This is key, because love, according to Paul, is how the body is built up and invigorated.

This is not a how-to book. There are already excellent resources on how to train a choir; how to teach simple three-part songs; guides on choosing repertoire; etc.[1] There are very few resources that focus on amateur musicians who have little to work with and provide them with a solid rationale for persevering. My aim is to fill that gap by framing that rationale in terms of Paul's metaphor of the body of Christ. Building the music scene in a church is deeply satisfying, but can also be gruelling. It requires stamina—emotionally and spiritually—and for that you need a clear idea of *why* you are doing it.

This book, as far as I can discern, is the first detailed attempt to relate Paul's metaphor of the body of Christ to the purpose of church music. Why focus on Paul? Firstly, Paul's writings have been central in shaping Christian theology and practice from the early Christian gatherings to the present day. Paul's thought is part of the DNA of the modern Christian church, so any study of the purpose of music within the church cannot avoid engaging with him. Secondly, Paul's overall vision of the body of Christ is as relevant and challenging today as it was for the early Christian communities.[2] It is a vision of a community that is grounded in love and a concern for others; where social, racial and gender differences are made irrelevant; where all are included in the worshipping life of the church and supported in their spiritual growth. These guiding principles ought to be fundamental for all those involved in church leadership, and by growing and managing the musical provision in our Christian community, we have a golden opportunity to apply them in a way that makes a tangible and significant difference.

Chapter 1 argues that a fundamental purpose of church music is to help build communities that are Christlike: a two-stage process, according to Paul, where (1) individuals are united into the body of Christ by the Spirit; and then (2) the body is built and invigorated by individuals acting in a loving and Christlike way towards one another. As Paul puts it succinctly, "love builds up".

Chapter 2 is focused on stage (1) and explores how participating in a nascent, developing choir enables an engagement with the Spirit, where "engagement with the Spirit" is understood in two ways. The first is what Paul referred to as "walking with the Spirit" which, for him, was an ethical command to change one's behaviour, attitude and outlook over time through an ongoing discipline. The second is the more direct, experiential engagement with the Spirit that is characteristic of Pentecostal and Charismatic churches.

Chapters 3 and 4 focus on stage (2). Chapter 3 looks within the existing worshipping community and explores how building a choir from scratch provides opportunities to achieve Paul's command to "discern the body of Christ": to enable everyone, in all their diversity, to participate in the worshipping life of the church.

Chapter 4 looks beyond the worshipping community and, partly in light of Paul's understanding of baptism, argues that a new, developing choir is well placed to engage those on the fringes or outside of the body of Christ.

Chapter 5 summarizes the main contentions of the book and explores its implications for the way church music is approached today.

Each chapter begins with a short vignette based on my experience at St John's that grounds and illustrates the reflection that follows it, and concludes with some questions for discussion that encourage the reader to apply the themes and suggestions to their own context.

St John's is part of the Church of England, and that is where most of my experience has been, but I hope it is clear how this book applies across denominations, and also to instrumental groups and other musical configurations, not just choirs.

1

Building the Body of Christ

It's Sunday morning and I'm struggling. Six are huddled around the piano for the pre-service rehearsal. That's about half the choir. Most of those turned up about ten minutes after we were due to start. Prior to the rehearsal, I had some tense words with a sidesperson about the proximity of the choir to the sanctuary, so I am already feeling out of sorts. One choir member is on particularly opinionated form and the men don't seem to know what page they should be looking at, despite me repeating "page two, bar ten" several times.

My normally solid façade of serenity and optimism is cracking.

Six months ago, I became musical director of St John's, Waterloo—the first in living memory. My first challenge was to pull together a choir for the Christmas Carol Service. I managed to muster a small but punchy group: Joyce and Rebecca from Sierra Leone, whose bright, forthright tones carried the tune; churchwarden David who provided a gentle tenor; and my girlfriend

Roz and local folk musician Kate who held a solid alto line. We sang two straightforward pieces: "Gaudete" and "I Saw Three Ships". It went fine. Not the most polished performance you've ever heard, but good enough for me to thank everyone afterwards with a genuine smile.

Since then, the choir has grown. David has managed to persuade his Portuguese wife Joao and youngest daughter Beatrix to join, and a modest influx of men has given David company on the tenor line and added a small bass section. We've sung a piece during Communion on a monthly basis—mostly simple chants from Taizé and Iona—rehearsing after the service on the preceding Sunday.[3] The standard is rather hit-and-miss, but overall choir pieces are sounding more confident. We've even attracted the occasional round of applause led by Holly—a particularly supportive nonagenarian who sits in the congregation.

When I remind myself of the difference compared to a few months ago, I am genuinely pleased (a "quantum leap" as Giles the vicar put it), but I am finding, more and more, that I have to prompt myself to think such positive thoughts. The adrenalin rush of starting something new is well and truly over and the week-by-week frustrations of running a church choir are coming to the fore.

I have chosen one of my favourites for the choir piece: the spiritual "Over My Head". It isn't sounding good. The refrain zips along with spirit and gusto, but the verses just sound messy. They are in a "call–response" format: Joyce provides the "call" (e.g. "Oh when I think on Jesus"), then the others are meant to respond, confidently and emphatically: "There is music in the air!" To complicate matters, while Joyce is singing, the others are meant to accompany her by "hmmm-ing" sustained notes, before breaking into the response line.

The sustained notes aren't sounding, let alone sustaining; and the response "There is music in the air!" is unsure and often late.

We have fifteen minutes to fix this.

Forget the sustained notes, I decide. Better they aren't there at all than half-there, sounding like we don't know what we're doing. The organist can play them (if I remember to tell him when he arrives). The response line, however, *must* be there. We spend as long as we can going over and over it, knowing full well that the congregation is arriving, listening to this.

Giles taps me on the shoulder. It's 10.30 a.m. We need to begin the first hymn.

The service is a mixed bag. The hymns and canticles are sung at a good pace—better than before the choir existed, when they dragged. One of the hymns, which we didn't manage to rehearse, is unfamiliar, and sounds very unsure. I end up singing it at the top of my voice, trying to gee-up the choir, to little effect. The emergency surgery we conducted on "Over My Head" works, in that the response line is delivered with more confidence than it was at the beginning of the rehearsal, but it's still a mile away from how it sounded in my head, just a couple of hours ago.

I tidy away after the service and head back to the flat, feeling frustrated. Part of me is wondering about the point of it all.

—

During the first few months at St John's, I struggled to get the sound from the choir that I thought they could produce. I also faced several logistical issues, such as finding a suitable location for the pre-service rehearsal.

I could feel myself getting more and more frustrated. It wasn't until, with the help of those around me, I was able to put the musical output in context and acknowledge the other, equally fundamental reasons we do what we do, that I reduced the pressure I was putting on myself and the choir.

Church music is about striving for musical results, but, as I will argue in this chapter, this isn't its only goal. A fundamental purpose of church music is to build the body of Christ—to transform individuals and the community to be more Christlike. Recognizing this as a musical director is very important, because it puts things in perspective when we are frustrated, and it is an essential check-and-balance when the music is sounding great.

Church music as facilitating worship, in the full, Pauline sense of "worship"

What is the point of church music? An obvious answer is that it facilitates worship. But what is worship and how, consequently, is music meant to facilitate it?

"Worship" is often understood to refer to the ritual activity that takes place in church, usually on a Sunday. Sometimes it is understood to refer merely to the singing bit of that ritual. However, both interpretations are arguably too narrow. Scripture—particularly the writings of St Paul in the New Testament—suggests an understanding of "worship" as something that encompasses one's whole life, not just that bit of it that happens in church on a pew.[4]

This is perhaps clearest in Paul's often-quoted opening to Romans 12:

> Therefore, I urge you, brothers and sisters, in view of
> God's mercy, to offer your bodies as a living sacrifice,
> holy and pleasing to God—this is your true and
> proper worship.
>
> *Romans 12:1*

By "bodies" is meant ourselves as a totality—all our thoughts, actions, habits, relationships, etc.—not just skin and bones. Ensuring that these are "holy and pleasing to God" is, according to Paul, acceptable worship. Worship is much more than the fraction of our lives that is confined to ritual or other church-based activities.

Paul goes on to explain in practical terms what counts as acceptable worship:

1. Using our gifts for the good of the whole community;
2. Ministering effectively to one another in love and forgiveness;
3. Living in a right relationship with governing authorities; and
4. Fostering understanding and unity particularly amongst those with differing opinions within the body of Christ (Romans 12–15).

A similar idea—that worship is something much broader than what happens during formal gatherings—is also present elsewhere in the New Testament. In Acts 2:42–47, Luke describes early Christian gatherings where those present would eat together and share their material blessings:

> They devoted themselves to the apostles' teaching and to fellowship, to the breaking of bread and to prayer. Everyone was filled with awe at the many wonders and signs performed by the apostles. All the believers were together and had everything in common. They sold property and possessions to give to anyone who had need. Every day they continued

to meet together in the temple courts. They broke bread in their homes and ate together with glad and sincere hearts, praising God and enjoying the favour of all the people. And the Lord added to their number daily those who were being saved.

The word "fellowship" in the first sentence is a rendering of the Greek word "*koinonia*" and doesn't really convey its full meaning. *Koinonia* certainly involves a relationship with others in the body of Christ—what Paula Gooder in *Body* refers to as its "horizontal" aspect—but it also involves what Gooder terms a "vertical" aspect, which is the individual's relationship with Christ.[5] The relationship between the early followers of Christ was deeper and more active than the term "fellowship" might imply: it was grounded in their faith in Christ and characterized by a sense of responsibility to one another. Tom Wright describes the bond between those devoting themselves to *koinonia* as so close that they "not only belong to one another but actually become mutually identified, truly rejoicing with the happy and genuinely weeping with the sad".[6]

This sort of relationship, if genuine, extends beyond formal gatherings, and is marked by actions we take and the way we live our lives, such as sharing our blessings and gifts with those in need. Indeed, formal gatherings such as that described above in the passage from Acts, where individuals would share their material blessings and eat together, feel like a practical expression of koinonia: of their relationship with each other and with Christ.[7] The gathering itself might be contained within a particular venue and timespan, but it is a symptom or natural consequence of something that extends far beyond, infusing the life of those who make up the body of Christ.

We are used to thinking of church music as something that facilitates church services and other, similar events when we gather as Christians. However, if a purpose of church music is to facilitate worship in the full, Pauline sense of "worship", it is meant to facilitate much more than what happens in church on a Sunday. In relation to 1) to 4) above, church music should, for instance:

1. Find ways of engaging *everyone* within the worshipping community, regardless of how musically talented or skilled they are, or what musical genre they naturally relate to. This means engaging individuals both as listeners and participants, and enabling the diversity of musical gifts in the community to flourish.

2. Contribute to pastoral work. Not in the sense of adding to pastoral caseload (as happens all too often), but in the sense of, for instance, offering a role and purpose to someone who is trying to find their feet by encouraging them into the choir or worship band.

3. Offer a way of reflecting on issues that ought to concern governing authorities. In a democracy,

part of being in a right relationship with governing authorities is to engage with them on issues that matter to you and those in your midst. Christian music can facilitate this, and has done so, over many years. There is a long tradition of Christian music expressing, for instance, the hope of freedom from oppression (e.g. traditional spirituals such as " Go Down Moses"; and contemporary hymns such as "Heaven Shall Not Wait" by John Bell).

4. Foster unity, within and beyond the worshipping community. This means using music to celebrate the diversity within the community, such as singing hymns that are distinctive to ethnic groups within the congregation; and to celebrate the diversity across the Christian community as a whole, such as contributing to ecumenical services.

One might object that the above is a linguistic sleight of hand; that when we say that church music facilitates worship, we are clearly using the term "worship" in a narrower sense, to mean the ritualistic activity that happens in Christian gatherings. However, and in response to this, understanding worship in this narrow way misses what is, for Paul, a fundamental purpose of it, which is to build Christlike communities. Consequently, church music really ought to concern itself with the musical gifts and diversity of the worshipping community, and seek opportunities to assist with pastoral work and political campaigning.

This is not least because, as I will argue throughout this book, church music is a very effective tool in building the sort of communities Paul had in mind.

Church music as an agent of transformation

Another helpful way to explore the purpose of church music is to reflect on Paul's statement that the church is the body of Christ. Taking this equivalence as given, we can say that *church* music is, in some sense, *body-of-Christ* music. I find this to be an incredibly useful way of thinking about church music. For instance, it brings home how, just as Christ's body was both in the world (people could touch, embrace and harm him) and yet transcendent of it (in that his body, in some sense, lives on); so church music is both this-worldly (it is a series of physical actions that create vibrations in the air) and yet enables its listeners to glimpse something beyond the everyday.

It also brings home how church music is an agent of transformation. To understand this, it is necessary to recall that by the "body of Christ", Paul meant that *the people who make up the church* are Christ's body. The church, for Paul, wasn't an institution or a set of buildings, but a group of people, formed into communities spanning a wide geographical area, who were continuing Christ's work. This involved transformation, both at the personal and community level. People had to work hard to grow into the body of Christ and to build it up, so that it could continue Christ's work effectively.

Understood this way, "church" music is not so much music that is associated with a particular institution or actions that take place in a particular sort of building, it is music that is *of* the people that make up the church. It is one of the activities we do to transform ourselves, and those around us, into the body of Christ.

So, those who are running and developing the music scene within a worshipping community are engaged in one of the principal aims (if not *the* principal aim) of the worldwide Christian Church: transforming individuals and communities to become the body of Christ. This is what distinguishes church music from the performance of sacred music in a concert setting, in that the latter does not involve attempting to form the listeners and performers into a unified whole that advances Christ's work on earth.[8]

In the following chapters, we will explore how, according to Paul, the body is knitted together, built up and invigorated, and attempt to discern how an amateur church musician, who is building something new with few resources, is contributing to this process. But beforehand, it would be useful to provide a quick overview of how this process works.

Paul's two-stage process to building the body of Christ

Paul seems to suggest that there is a two-stage process to forming and developing the body of Christ.[9] Firstly, we are all formed into the body of Christ by the Spirit. The Spirit is the active ingredient that binds the body together. How? There is some sense in which we receive and experience the Spirit. Paul expresses this to the Corinthian community in terms of being baptized in the Spirit and drinking it:

> For we were all baptized by [or 'in' or 'with'] one Spirit so as to form one body—whether Jews or Gentiles, slave or free—and we were all given the one Spirit to drink.
>
> *1 Corinthians 12:13*

Exactly what sort of experience(s) this refers to is the source of much dispute. Some argue that "baptize" here refers to the sacrament of baptism and that Paul is describing two, separate experiences of the Spirit: one at baptism and the other at Communion (hence the use of the verb "to drink"). Others argue that Paul's language is metaphorical and that he is referring to a single experience: the Corinthians' common experience of conversion.[10] Wherever one stands on these disputes, it is natural to suppose that, regardless of whatever else Paul has in mind, he is describing the receipt of spiritual sustenance, and it is this sustenance that plays a fundamental role in knitting the body of Christ together.[11]

Secondly, the body of Christ, once it has been formed, must be built up. For Paul, being formed into a unity by the Spirit is just the beginning. The members of that unity must then work to grow and invigorate it. How? Paul's answer is straightforward: love builds up (1 Corinthians 8:1); love is "the most excellent way" (1 Corinthians 12:31); and that means acting as Christ did.[12] It means putting the interests of others above self-interest and demonstrating the selfless love that is exemplified by Christ on the cross.

Paul applies this to a specific situation in the Corinthian community (1 Corinthians 13–14). The Corinthians' use of *charismata* (or "spiritual gifts") was, for Paul, not indicative of an approach with love at its core. Paul felt that their use of tongues was overzealous and, unless interpreted by someone so the whole community could understand what was being said, edified the individual only (the one speaking in tongues). A loving approach, and the one that Paul urged, would be to ensure that the whole community is edified. Consequently, Paul petitions the Corinthians to choose prophesy over tongues, because it tends to be delivered in normal speech.[13]

Understanding church music as contributing to this two-stage process complements the suggestion, outlined above, that it ought to facilitate the full Pauline sense of "worship". In developing the musical skills of the whole community, irrespective of ability or musical preference, we are edifying the whole community, rather than a select few. Furthermore, as I will argue in the next chapter, we are furnishing individuals with another way in which they can engage with the Spirit—the fundamental agent, according to Paul, that knits the body together. By contributing to pastoral work and fostering unity within and beyond the community, we are encouraging the body of Christ to act in a loving, open and inclusive way which, in Paul's view, will best enable the body to grow and be invigorated. Similarly, although not always the case, the political views expressed by many hymns and songs in the Christian tradition draw our attention away from ourselves and towards the oppressed and ignored.

Church music as building the body of Christ

The upshot of the above is that church music is not just about making a beautiful sound. A fundamental purpose is its role in building the body of Christ. Whether a choir or instrumental group is producing a beautiful sound bears little relation to whether it is helping or hindering the process of developing a Christlike community. Indeed, frustrating rehearsals like that described at the beginning of this chapter, where half the choir is absent and the other half can't seem to find the right page, can be an indicator that our focus is exactly where it should be: on the community, as much as on the notes. For in building a choir from the congregation, we are creating something with in-built links back into the congregation that spark repertoire choices, develop the musical gifts of the community, and instil a fresh sense that the community itself has something musical to offer. However, we are also dealing with human beings from all walks of life, who wouldn't naturally consider themselves as "musicians", and who might or might not have appreciated that singing in a choir requires significant dedication.

As I found at St John's, it will go wrong sometimes, and it will be frustrating, but that is often a sign that we are doing exactly what we ought to be doing as church musicians: developing and invigorating the body of Christ. Conversely, if it's all feeling rather comfortable and easy, that can be a bad sign. It is never easy to find a way of enabling the whole community to develop their musical gifts. There is always a difficult balance between inclusion and quality of sound, and once it's struck, like a spinning top balanced on its point, it never remains so for long; and that can be because, for example, when it is going "well" and the choir is sounding beautiful, less-able choir members leave because they feel they can't keep up.

Moreover, by focusing on the community, we can be guided to make better musical decisions. Instead of putting yourself (or the music) at the centre of those decisions, your focus naturally broadens to the individuals in the worshipping community you are serving. For example, fostering unity requires understanding the diversity within the community in all its various forms—cultural, socio-economic, theological, etc.—and this understanding can be invaluable in picking repertoire that grabs the choir, ignites their imagination, and draws out their best. It was through exploring Sierra Leone National Day with the Sierra Leoneans at St John's that we landed on the idea of singing a psalm in Krio on the relevant Sunday, and it flew. In contrast, I found that picking my own favourites, perhaps with a nod to the general theme of the service, might or might not work.

It is also more likely, depending on the personalities involved, that fostering unity in this way will lead to a more constructive relationship with the clergy. The often-difficult relationship between musical director and clergy is well documented.[14] One cause of this that has been noted in previous studies is the lack of common ground between clergy and musicians. As Robin Rees' now dated but fascinating and relevant study *Weary and Ill at Ease* puts it, "The clergy had little knowledge of, or ability in, music . . . , whilst the directors' knowledge of theology was very limited."[15] Furthermore, Rees found that the clergy's view of the ideal musical director differed significantly from the musical director's view: the latter tended to prioritize musical skills (such as hymn-playing, choir-training, etc.) whereas the clergy mixed in other skills (such as pastoral gifts and liturgical awareness). In short, " . . . the directors were looking for specialist musicians, the clergy for all-rounders".[16]

Clergy of course need to do their bit to understand the challenges and possibilities faced by musical directors, by setting aside time for regular meetings; attending courses designed to this end such as the RSCM's *Inspiring Music in Worship*; and so on. However, if, as musical director, our focus shifts away from the purely musical aspects of our role and more towards understanding and facilitating the role of music in building the body of Christ, it would at least land us on ground where a meaningful conversation between musician and clergy is more likely.

Questions for discussion

How would you describe the aim of the musical provision in your worshipping community? How do you think that aim would be described by:

1. a choir member (or someone involved in providing the music);
2. the musical director;
3. a member of the congregation (who is not involved in providing the music);
4. a member of the clergy;
5. a visitor?

For each of the above, how does your answer compare to the suggestion that a fundamental purpose of church music is to facilitate worship (in the full, Pauline sense of "worship") and to build the body of Christ?

2

Engaging with the Spirit

It's a warm Sunday afternoon in June: the final day
of the Waterloo Festival, which climaxes with Choral
Evensong. St John's Choir will join with a large, robed
choir from the curate's home church: St Thomas-on-the-
Bourne, Farnham. They will each sing a piece (St John's
taking the introit; St Thomas' the anthem) and combine
for the hymns, psalm and responses.

I survey the choirs at the pre-service rehearsal. St
Thomas' has fielded the men, boys and girls only; the
ladies form a separate choir and "have decided to sit
this one out", so I am told. Neatly presented in their
purple robes, they are arranged in three rows of twenty
and appear like a sea of purple compared to St John's
Choir, who are tacked onto the left in three rows of four,
looking somewhat intimidated.

We sing through the hymns to warm up. The sound
mixes surprisingly well. The forthright tone of the St
John's sopranos adds some extra fizz to the top line.
The resonant sound of the St Thomas' men gives their

St John's counterparts extra impetus, resulting in a few more decibels than normal.

Next, each choir rehearses its own pieces. We go first with an energetic rendition of the South African chant "Bambelela", delivered with such confidence and joyful abandon that it mesmerizes some of the younger members of St Thomas'. Satisfied and just a little bit proud, I hand over to St Thomas' Director of Music who remarks favourably on the "bang for buck" and challenges everyone in his choir to commit in the same way. They set about rehearsing Tallis' "A New Commandment".

After the service, St Thomas' Choir disappears into their coach for the return journey. One member of St John's congregation, who is genuinely over the moon with the event, suggests to me that we might consider a formal link between the two choirs. St John's could learn so much, he says.

I smile politely and nod, non-committal.

Ouch.

I'm in little doubt that the individual meant well. It would also be true to say that I had developed a defensive streak when it came to St John's Choir. We had been through thick and thin together, even at this early stage. We had salvaged choir pieces from the abyss shortly before singing them to the gathered masses. Ours was a relationship forged in battle—not with each other, but with the music that we set out to tackle. I had grown rather fond of them.

Well, I think to myself, we don't sound like the choir from St Thomas'. That much is true. Our voices don't blend like theirs. We do not offer a pure, shimmering sound. One that has been tidied and made neat by years of moulding. Ours is more robust and rough around the edges. Gritty, even.

But, in a way, I don't mind the fact that certain voices stick out: that I can sometimes hear Joyce protruding from the sopranos, and David too when he gets excited. I even like the way the different accents make for vowels that don't entirely blend.

In short, I appreciate hearing the harmony *and* the distinctive voices that comprise it. I like having both, because it reminds me of an ideal: one that affirms individuality and community at the same time. And because it isn't neat and tidy—because you can tell that these individuals have not been smoothed out by years of training—the whole thing feels *authentic*, like the people really are coming together to pour forth in song. And my goodness, on a good day, they can sing with such spirit and energy.

I'm not sure precisely what the individual meant by his comment. I probably should have asked. But I wouldn't want to remove *all* the grit and rough edges. They are the secret ingredients that make what we are doing profoundly meaningful.

Walking with the Spirit

Church music is often said to facilitate an engagement with or experience of the Spirit. For example, Paul's letter to the Ephesians[17] associates singing with being "filled" with the Spirit:

> . . . be filled with the Spirit, speaking to one another with psalms, hymns, and songs from the Spirit. Sing and make music from your heart to the Lord, always giving thanks to God the Father for everything, in the name of our Lord Jesus Christ.
>
> *Ephesians 5:18–20*

Ethnomusicologist Mary McGann spent four years studying the musical and liturgical practices of Our Lady of Lourdes: a predominantly African American Catholic community in San Francisco. The music she encountered was in the gospel idiom, performed by choir, instrumentalists and other members of the community. McGann found that members of the community consider music to be key in enabling them to engage with the Spirit:

> Music is said to "wake up the Spirit," to allow the Spirit to "heal burdens," and to "bring surrender to God."[18]

Similar sentiments would be typical of worship in the Pentecostal and Charismatic movements in the UK and beyond, where such phenomena as singing in tongues are understood by the community as actions of the Spirit.[19] Although not as readily associated with the direct actions of the Spirit, music in churches with the more traditional choir-plus-organ set-up is often considered to enable a glimpse of the divine, or to lift one out of the everyday and into a different place, and even to change one's life.[20]

In the previous chapter, we saw how, for Paul, individuals are united into the body of Christ by the Spirit. Exactly how this happens is unclear, but Paul seems to describe individuals experiencing and receiving the Spirit ("drinking" the Spirit) which, at the very least, seems to suggest the receipt of spiritual sustenance. Consequently, by enabling an experience of or engagement with the Spirit, there is potential for church music to enable the first stage of building the body of Christ.

However, such sentiments are most readily associated with high-end, rather than developing musical scenes: a robed choir singing a glorious anthem in a building boasting fine architecture and evocative acoustics; or a polished praise band in a giant arena with immersive lighting and other effects. The sort of music that thrills, transports you to another place and perhaps even finds its way into your bones will differ depending on taste, but what is sure is that a middle-of-the-road, "average" parish church with one organist and a hymn book and a nascent choir of undisciplined singers is not what comes to mind when envisaging church musical set-ups that deliver a closer engagement with the Spirit!

This depends, of course, on what is meant by "engaging with the Spirit". The sort of engagement outlined above is in the form of immediate experiences that are accompanied by actions such as speaking in tongues ("glossolalia"). This sort of direct, experiential engagement was also presupposed by Paul, who considered glossolalia to be a "gift" of the Spirit (1 Corinthians 12–14). However, another understanding of what it might be to engage with the Spirit that is rooted in Paul's writings focuses not on immediate experiences, but on a much longer, sustained effort by the individual and their worshipping community. Paul uses the phrase "walk with the Spirit" on a number of occasions as an ethical command: one that means to act towards others in love; to seek to behave as Christ did.[21] This, for Paul, is the surest way of building the body of Christ: as we have already seen, according to Paul, love builds up.

Rowan Williams picks up on a similar understanding when he describes the Spirit as kindling a yearning within us to be fully and truly human; as engaging the "quivering magnetic needle" within us that points north, to what we are meant to be.[22] This, Williams argues, is a humanity that embraces others and seeks to remove injustice and inequality:

> And that's a humanity that does not break down into powerful and powerless, rich and poor; it is a humanity in which everybody's poverty and need is affirmed and recognized; everybody's need of one another is recognized.[23]

This sort of engagement with the Spirit is about changing attitudes, outlook and behaviour through a prolonged discipline. As the phrase suggests, "walking with the Spirit" is about gradual, deliberate progress, putting one foot after the other. Experiences of music in church of the more direct, experiential sort will undoubtedly help by providing profound spiritual sustenance, inspiring one to persevere, but they won't be sufficient on their own. Walking with the Spirit is about action—about acting one's way into thinking, rather than thinking one's way into acting. Like riding a bike or playing the piano, only by practising and inhabiting the way Christ acted towards others can one begin to do the same, naturally and without deliberate, corrective thought.

When Holly—the particularly supportive nonagenarian—returned to church following hip surgery, St John's Choir heralded her recovery by singing one of her favourites: an ingenious medley consisting of the spirituals "O When the Saints", "I'm Gonna Sing", "Rollin' Along" and "Swing Low, Sweet Chariot", all sung on top of each other. Church music can be used in straightforwardly pastoral ways, which in turn helps to create an ethos that is caring and attentive to others.

However, it runs deeper than this. As Steven Guthrie suggests, the very act of singing in a choir, whether or not the focus is something pastoral, can instil the sort of Christlike behaviour that ought to characterize the unified church.[24] Although he doesn't explicitly refer to Paul's command to "walk with the Spirit", the sort of behaviour Guthrie describes would undoubtedly chime with what Paul had in mind.[25]

For example, singers within a choir submit to each other, in that they all synchronize to a common tempo and rhythm, melody and key. Singers "make room" for other singers, allowing them to stand out as needed by the music, rather than trying to drown them out. This is despite the fact that, as Daniel Barenboim points out, another voice might even "contradict" your own, such as by sounding a clashing note.[26] As Guthrie explains, "In a multi-voiced harmony, privileging some voices and excluding others does not mean that the louder voices 'win'. Rather, the harmony as a whole fails."[27]

Making room for other singers instils a sensitivity to others, in that one actively listens to what others are doing and responds accordingly, adjusting tone, volume, tempo and rhythm (amongst a myriad of other variables) to blend into the chorus. Guthrie argues that, in doing so, we are reminded that "there are others in the room, that the people seated to my right and to my left have voices"; and that "in these instances we *indwell* a kind of sensitivity and responsiveness to others".[28]

Like the demands of living in and building a community, submitting and being sensitive to others when singing in a choir requires adhering to constraints, where those constraints do not oppress but open possibilities: in this case, the possibility of singing together in harmony.[29]

Guthrie focuses on the demands of singing in *any* choir. However, the behaviour he outlines was especially required at St John's where the choir was new and developing, and comprised mostly of individuals who were not trained musicians or experienced singers. They had to listen and work harder to blend their voices, which had not been smoothed and moulded by training and long experience of singing in choirs. Keeping together—ensuring that you don't end up two beats ahead of the tenors, for instance—wasn't yet second nature and required a conscious effort to stay in line. Those who were very capable or experienced had to keep their wits about them: they had to realize when they were being relied upon by others for a tricky entry or difficult passage, shoulder the extra responsibility, and make sure they were on the money.

Glimpsing an alternative reality

So, understood as a longer-term walk with the Spirit, singing in a developing choir facilitates an engagement with the Spirit, and even more so because of the extra demands that result from it being a developing choir. This is yet another example of a profound benefit that is easy to ignore when you're stressed about the next musical thing to fix.

At the beginning of this chapter, I described the more direct, experiential "engagement with the Spirit" that is associated with high-end music in church. Is this really beyond a choir in a similar stage of development as St John's?

What many of the more direct, experiential engagements with the Spirit have in common is the sense of a closer connection with the divine: with a reality that transcends this one and is profoundly greater than it. The gifts of glossolalia and prophesy in the Pentecostal and Charismatic movements, for example, are understood by the gathered community as mystical encounters with God.[30]

We have already seen how singing in a developing choir helps to bring about some of that new reality, by nudging individuals towards adopting a more Christlike way of acting towards each other. What I would like to suggest now is that it also enables a visceral sense—a glimpse—of what that alternative reality could be like.

The experience of singing in harmony can be striking, particularly when it is a relatively new experience. It can be a simple piece such as a Taizé chant or African American spiritual. It doesn't even have to be spotless in its execution. As Guthrie puts it, by inhabiting the harmony—by being part of it, standing near those who are providing the other notes—you hear your own voice, the voices of others, and "this third thing—our voices together: a sound which has properties which belong neither to your voice nor to my voice alone, but one that is nevertheless shaped and takes its substance from the individual voices comprising it".[31] You are hit with a powerful sense—what Guthrie refers to as a "sounding image"—of the community that is joining together in voice: diverse yet unified; shaped by the individuals that comprise it, but greater than the sum of its parts.[32]

Singing together in unison can deliver a strong sense of community and solidarity with others, as many who attend football matches or local pub sings can attest. Similarly with unison singing in church: McGann found that participants at Our Lady of Lourdes felt a keen sense of communion during extended periods of song.[33] Singing in harmony seems to deliver the same, but with added dimensions. While I was preparing to write this book, I asked Shanon to describe his experience of singing in harmony. Shanon achieved some success as a singer-songwriter in Malaysia before moving to the UK to study for a PhD. He had never sung a harmony line before joining St John's Choir:

> When I sang in harmony for the first time at St John's, it really gave me a sense of humility and magic at the same time. I felt so pleased at being able to make this sound, to contribute to the richness of the music, and yet also humbled that I was but one voice amongst many making this happen. It contrasted so much with my previous experience as a solo singer-songwriter, who had to make sure my voice carried the performance and that I had to be the 'star'. I felt like a brushstroke in a lovely oil painting. Or a twinkling star in the night sky. It was that lovely feeling of knowing you're special and that you've helped to make something wonderful happen, and also that everyone else there was special, too.

You might think you're expendable as part of the harmony, certainly compared to a soloist. But you're not. You're an essential part of something beautiful and creative—the sound of many voices in harmony—that cannot exist in the same way without you. Indeed, take one voice away from a group singing in harmony and the effect is likely to be much greater than if the same group was singing in unison, particularly if there are just one or two on each harmony line.

Even if not expendable, you might think that you're somehow lost in the mix when singing in harmony; that you're blended into homogeneity. Stacy Horn, whose book *Imperfect Harmony* explores her experience of singing in the Choral Society of Grace Church in New York, suggests the opposite:

> The difference between unison singing and the expansion into harmony is the same as the difference between love and the absence of love. You don't disappear within the group (or person) when you've found harmony (or love), you become more present and reverberatingly alive.[34]

It is as if you find yourself—your own voice—in and through the activity of others. Particularly if you are singing harmony notes (rather than the tune) there is a very clear sense in which this is so, since your notes are incomplete and even ambiguous without the other notes that make up the harmony. Only in the context of those other notes can you tell whether you are, for example, filling out the harmony with no sense of leaning towards your next note, or whether you are part of a discord that needs to resolve. And yet, finding yourself through others in this way does not diminish your individuality; your distinctiveness. On the contrary: it is because the note you are sounding differs to those around you that harmony can exist.

In short, singing in harmony provides a direct experience of what it is to affirm community and individuality in equal measure. This is an experience of exactly the sort of community that Paul had in mind. Paul likens the body of Christ to a human body, and individuals within it to parts of that body, such as its hands, head and feet (1 Corinthians 12:14–31). For Paul, this isn't just a matter of an individual's function within the body, but also their identity: being a member of the body is part of who they are. This is why, as Paul suggests in verse 26, "If one part suffers, every part suffers with it; if one part is honoured, every part rejoices with it." An affliction against any member of the body of Christ is also an affliction against me; a joy felt by any member is also a joy felt by me.[35] Yet, just as harmony relies on diversity and individuality for its very existence, so does the body of Christ.[36]

Freedom and spontaneity

Another commonality between worship styles that are considered to "engage with the Spirit" is that there is a level of freedom and spontaneity. McGann's study of the community in Lourdes found that space was made for musical improvisation, the product of which was connected directly to the actions of the Spirit.[37] There are other, more subtle ways this is done in traditions that perhaps do not make such a direct association, such as leaving open how many times a Taizé chant is repeated, or improvising an alternative harmony on the organ for the final verse of a hymn.

There is a way in which voluntary, developing church music scenes are free and spontaneous. They can be chaotic. At St John's, it was very rarely the case that the whole choir was there for any given rehearsal, often to the extent that I was presented with a different choir week by week. I was never *absolutely* sure how it was going to sound Sunday by Sunday, or if it was even going to work. Yet, somehow, despite the chaos and unreliability, more often than not it came good, and in ways I couldn't predict. There were occasions where I changed the choir piece ten minutes before the Sunday morning rehearsal because (say) no men had turned up, and found that the revised choice worked better than the original choice would have done. At least once, I drafted in an unsuspecting newcomer to bolster the men, who then found their home in the choir. It is as if running a voluntary, grass-roots church choir has an inbuilt need for spontaneity, which is grasped and wielded for good by something—whether that "something" is identified with the Spirit; or the inner, spiritual reality of the worshipping community; or something else.

Erik Routley grounds his approach to church music in what he refers to as the New Testament principle of grace, which is that one ought to focus on the generation of good rather than the avoidance of error.[38] According to that principle, it is not enough to be blameless in the eye of the law, such as by ensuring that you walk at least one mile with someone who obliges you to carry their pack. Rather, you must seek to extend the goodness of your action by walking another mile, as an act of grace.[39] Paul similarly felt that focusing too much on keeping to rules (in his context, those set out in the Torah) is not a particularly effective way of bringing about a righteous life. This is why Paul turned to the Spirit instead of Torah as the ultimate guide to right and wrong.[40]

This is sound advice for any musician. I certainly find it to be a useful state of mind to train oneself into before playing the organ or conducting a choir: somehow, by worrying less about mistakes, fewer mistakes happen, everyone is more relaxed, and the final product is more effective. This is *essential* advice for those involved in building voluntary church choirs from the grass roots, because any approach that focuses too heavily on fault-finding is going to smother spontaneity, and will probably result in a frustrated musical director and dispirited set of musicians, if anyone is left. In contrast, by focusing on the good generated by church-music-making—musical and non-musical—we are more able to embrace the need for spontaneity, and make room for the unexpected.

Questions for discussion

Describe any ways in which making music with others (such as singing in a choir or congregation, or playing in an instrumental group) has changed your behaviour, attitude and outlook. Describe any ways in which this has happened to others—particularly those in your worshipping community.

How would you describe the experience of singing in harmony? How does it compare to the way you interact with others in everyday life? (If you haven't experienced singing in harmony, but have experienced singing or playing alongside others, describe that instead.)

What opportunities does your worshipping community provide for people to sing together? Think of some creative ways in which these could be developed or additional opportunities offered, to include giving people the chance to experience harmony.

Is freedom and spontaneity characteristic, to *any* extent (however large or small, intended or unintended), of the musical provision offered by your community? If not, think of some ways in which it could be introduced. If so, what does that freedom and spontaneity lead to (including the good and the challenging)?

3

Discerning the Body of Christ

It's Holly's (the particularly supportive nonagenarian) ninety-second birthday. In characteristic style, she organizes a banquet for after the Sunday service. Sandwiches and wraps of various sorts; crisps and crudités; buckets of sparkling wine are purchased and tidied away in the kitchen ready for the big day. Holly picks her favourite hymns for the service and asks a friend, who happens to be a professional countertenor, to sing a solo.

Holly loves a good party. A series of hip operations has left her largely confined to a wheelchair, but that did not stop her from dancing at the big tea party at last year's Community Festival. She is famous for wearing a decorated disposable bedpan as a hat for the Queen's Jubilee. Holly's big, friendly eyes twinkle with a youthfulness that belies her age: a vibrancy that is also reflected in her typical attire, which is invariably bright purple with an African twist (normally a fez)—the latter a nod to her many years spent living in Nigeria, married to a prince.

Yes, Holly married a Nigerian prince. And not just any prince—her husband was heir to the Osogbo throne. "My father-in-law the king," Holly is fond of dropping into conversations. It wasn't as glamorous as you might think: Holly had to move around in Nigeria quite a bit and describes her time there as lonely. She was relieved to return to the UK.

Nevertheless, it isn't every day that you meet a Nigerian princess, especially one with a broad Sheffield accent.

Holly's support for the choir has been unwavering. She often leads a round of applause following a particularly rousing anthem, and she has persisted in telling me—to my face and *super embarrassingly* announcing it during the notices at the end of the service—just how wonderful the choir is. I regard Holly with a mix of deep gratitude and fear of what she might say next.

The day of the party arrives. I turn up early as per normal to set up chairs and run through the service sheet before the rehearsal. The 9 a.m. congregation is finishing breakfast. The chatter is noticeably quiet and subdued, which I fleetingly clock as odd, but my focus is on the chairs and the music. The choir will be arriving shortly, and there's always a surprise to sort, like a hymn printed with half a verse missing.

The vicar pops over. Holly died in hospital last night.

I am not, it would be fair to say, someone who wears their emotions on their sleeve. Indeed, an old friend once quipped that I have one emotion—consciousness—which, last time I checked, isn't an emotion at all. It is situations where the pressure is on to *show* an emotion that I dread the most, which includes this one. It is regretful to report, therefore, that my immediate reaction to the news of Holly's passing is not shock or sadness, but embarrassment. Not quite knowing what to say, I turn to what I know best and what I was usefully thinking about anyway just moments ago: the music.

"We shouldn't change a thing," I say. "Music and party and the whole caboodle. Holly wanted a party. We should throw her a party."

The choir gradually dribbles in and learns the sad news. Joyce, who was particularly close to Holly and helped with cleaning her flat, shopping for essentials and pushing her wheelchair to church, is in tears. Everyone else is silent with shock.

I explain the plan. Not a note will be changed. Today is a celebration of life, just as Holly intended it. Somehow, we need to put our emotions to one side and sing the upbeat music with the same joyfulness as if Holly is there. There will be plenty of time for grieving afterwards.

We set about rehearsing and take our seats ready for the service to begin.

The first hymn is "Immortal, Invisible", which I normally prefer to be sung strongly at a reasonable pace.

I conduct it accordingly. Despite my best efforts, the sound feels small and weak, as if broken. The Gloria, which is short and simple (a catchy tune sung by the ladies with a fun line for men: Iona at its best), lacks any of its spark and energy, despite the best efforts of the organist and determined aerobics by me. It's the choir's turn to lead the responsorial psalm, which I approach with quiet and hidden dread given our performance so far. We get through it. Just.

I begin to wonder if I've made the right decision. Not everyone buries their emotions like I do. Perhaps I should have swapped some of the more upbeat pieces for reflective ones.

The soloist sings "I wonder as I wander out under the sky" beautifully; the sense of a mysterious journey chimes with thoughts about Holly's new adventure into the ultimate unknown. Thank goodness something musical has gone right in this service, I think to myself.

The final hymn is Holly's favourite: "O when the Saints". I approach it as per the other upbeat hymns in the service. No pulling back. Full throttle. It hasn't really worked thus far, but I know of no other way to sing it apart from with gusto, and Holly would not have been impressed with anything less. Come on people, let's make this one fly.

We work our way through the verses. "O when the saints go marching in . . . ; O when they crown him Lord of all . . . ; O when all knees bow at His name . . . ; O when they sing the Saviour's praise . . . ". Although lacking its normal jollity, the sound picks up. I put it down to relief that the service is almost over.

It takes until the last verse, which is a repeat of the first: "O when the saints go marching in ... ". Joyce spontaneously starts to sing "Swing Low, Sweet Chariot" over the top, inspired by the medley we sang for Holly when she returned from hip surgery. Rebecca and a few other choir members join in. David, who realizes exactly what Joyce and Rebecca are doing, breaks into "Rollin' Along, Singin' this Song". As it builds, Joyce and Rebecca begin to clap and dance. The atmosphere in church brightens. I can feel the emotional tension in the church releasing, as if a pressure valve has been opened.

The last verse nears an end, but I don't want it to stop. I signal to the choir and organist to keep going. "O when the Saints! O when the Saints! O when the Saints go marching in ... ". Everyone is singing and—to various degrees—moving, clapping, dancing.

What a glorious moment.

Enabling participation

We lead messy emotional lives. Our emotions can be chaotic. They come and go without warning. They aren't always understandable, such as my fear of swimming, which I can't explain. They conflict with each other. Music might not be able to solve all of this, but a range of literature argues that it can help us to order and express our emotions.

For example, according to the theologian and musician Jeremy Begbie, music can help us to focus on one emotion (rather than fail to cope with four or five all vying for our attention).[41] Begbie likens the way music represents emotion to the gestures of a dancer. By deploying movements such as a glare, clenched fist, or thrust of the head, dancers are able to distinguish between emotions and represent one at a time, such as anger or grief. Similarly, through melody, ornaments such as appoggiaturas and other devices, music is able to offer (for example) "concentrated grief" and even distinguish between different sorts of grief.[42] Begbie argues that this can transform our emotional involvement with something by "purifying, compressing and specifying our emotions". For instance, by helping an individual or a group to focus on grief at a funeral or joy at a service that celebrates a life that was long and full, they are able to remove all other distractions and grieve (or celebrate) more deeply.

Jonathan Arnold argues that sacred music is something that by nature invokes a "creative and participatory" response, and indeed Arnold's suggestion rings true.[43] When singing "Abide with Me" there is a sense in which I am not just relaying a text that requests guidance in dark times; I am, myself, asking for that guidance. When singing "When I Needed a Neighbour, Were You There"

I'm not just describing the cries of the oppressed and forgotten, but adding my cry to theirs. The point is that you're doing more than simply expressing an emotion. When singing a hymn or song you are not just expressing praise, but praising; not just expressing joy, but really celebrating. There is a difference: a skilled actor can express praise or joy, much like a dancer can express anger, without truly praising or experiencing genuine joy or anger.

Put the two together—the way music enables the individual and the group to focus on a particular emotion; and the way it enables us to participate in a shared act of praise or grief or celebration—and you have a powerful combination. For it enables the group to begin to process events that have a significant impact on the community.

Take, for example, the death of a much-loved member. Such an event can leave people grappling with conflicting emotions: grief and sadness might be mixed with gratitude for a life that was long and full, or relief that a painful decline has finally found peace. The first time everyone gathers after the event and discovers the news, the subdued atmosphere can be as much people not knowing how to act and express what they're thinking, as it will be sadness. Music—whether something performed by choir or instrumental group or a congregational hymn—can catch a shared emotion and bring it to the fore, disentangling it from all the others. It can draw the people present into a shared response, through singing the hymn, or simply listening to the music and feeling that it expresses what you and those standing near and next to you were really trying to say.[44]

When the choir leading the hymn or singing the choir-only piece is drawn from the congregation, its ability to facilitate such a response from the congregation is enhanced, because the line between choir and congregation is especially blurred. The choir comprises individuals who, for the most part, would attend even if the choir didn't exist; who are friends and relatives of individuals who don't count themselves as part of the choir; who often have roles additional to "choir member", such as treasurer or member of the environmental group or coordinator of the tea-towel-washing rota. Watching these individuals, with whom you already have non-musical connections of various sorts, spark on a musical response such as remembering that "Swing Low" harmonizes beautifully with "O When the Saints" (and speaks of finding peace through death), is far more likely to move you into sharing in that response.

Embracing diversity and unifying the community

Ensuring all are able to express—in a very real, participatory sense—their worries and joys is an essential part of ensuring that all are in involved and included within the worshipping life of the church. Paul was also very concerned about this, as shown in his advice to the Corinthians (1 Corinthians 11:17–34). According to Paul, the haves conducted the Lord's Supper in a way that humiliated and excluded the have-nots, by conducting their own "private suppers" and allowing the have-nots to go hungry. Paul's request was that the haves "discern the body of Christ"; that is, recognize and include everyone, including the have-nots.[45]

Paul's aim was to create unities that are inclusive of everyone in the body of Christ, rather than sub-groupings that include some and exclude others. This is part of the second stage of building the body of Christ. As outlined in Chapter 1, individuals are initially united into the body of Christ by the Spirit, but for Paul this is just the beginning. The next stage is for individuals to adopt a loving and Christlike way of behaving towards others, which will enable the body to be invigorated and built up. Ensuring that everyone is included in the worshipping life of the community is a key example of Christlike behaviour.

By enabling inclusive worship, church music is contributing to this second stage of building the body of Christ. However, in practice it doesn't always work out like that.

We are reasonably adept at producing musical scenes that unify. The experience of those playing in a praise band or singing in a choir can include intense solidarity with the other participants. This powerful sense of solidarity can extend to listeners, reinforced in modern worship by immersive lights and other effects. Similarly, the more traditional choir-plus-organ set-up and the style of worship that often comes with it (e.g. Choral Evensong) can be key to how someone identifies with a worshipping community, perhaps because they grew up with it and enjoy the familiarity of the structure and words, or even sang it themselves as a child chorister.

Although unifying, such musical scenes can also be very exclusive. The very act of creating a choir or instrumental group means separating, to some degree, a group of people from the congregation. This can create a sense of elitism and convince people who are not in the choir or instrumental group that their musical talents aren't good enough to offer in worship.[46] Natural bonds that are formed between musicians can lead to intimidation at breaking into what can come across as an established, closed micro-community. The familiarity of a distinctive musical tradition such as Choral Evensong is welcoming "home turf" to some but alien to others, and a reminder of how they don't "fit" with this musical scene.

There is a difficult balance to strike. We want musical scenes that unify: that strengthen communities by offering a sonic landscape that unlocks emotions which are shared by all who are gathered, such as grief in response to the death of one of its members; and that build bridges and bonds between individuals and enable them to find a home in their worshipping community. But we also need to keep those communities open, outward-looking and inclusive of the diversity within them which, as we have already seen, is essential for the mere existence of the body, let alone its growth and development.

Developing a choir or instrumental group does not automatically lead to an exclusive music scene. On the contrary, it can be a way of making a community's approach to music more inclusive. Valuing a diversity of individuals means actively involving them in the musical life of the worshipping community and celebrating, rather than smoothing over, the differences. To this end, in being asked to build a choir at St John's, I was given a wonderful opportunity. For I didn't have to conform to an ongoing tradition, such as a particular style or repertoire, but I could build the repertoire and ethos of the choir around those within it and around the needs of the congregation, using the existing links between the choir and congregation. This automatically helped to draw out and give voice to the diversity within the worshipping community. For example, many of the nationalities in the congregation at St John's were represented in the choir, which provided an excellent excuse—and a first-hand source of knowledge—to explore international repertoire and celebrate cultural events in song during worship (e.g. singing a psalm in Krio to mark Sierra Leone National Day). It also brought distinctive musical gifts, such as forthright, vibrant singing voices; a culturally-generated ability to improvise harmony; and a natural sense of musical scales that are less common in the UK (e.g. pentatonic scales—characteristic of Korean music, which was home for one regular choir member).

We have already seen how music enables us to engage with the Spirit, even when the choir is nascent and developing, as at St John's. In Genesis we find the powerful image of the creator Spirit that brooded above the formless world before it began to take shape:

> In the beginning God created the heavens and the earth. Now the earth was formless and empty, darkness was over the surface of the deep, and the Spirit of God was hovering over the waters.
>
> *Genesis 1:1–2*

Church music, when it is done in a way that builds the body of Christ, forms and shapes our worshipping communities. It helps us to draw out and articulate the contours within them—not just nationalities, cultural backgrounds and musical abilities but also theological leanings and political and social concerns, to name but a few. Once these are articulated, they can be used to inform, for instance, a theme on which to focus during Lent, or a style of worship to explore. This not only helps to produce worship that is fresh and relevant to the congregation; it also enables individuals to worship on their own terms, in their own way. You allow them to be themselves—to bring their whole being, flesh, bones, personality flaws and the rest, to God in worship, just as Paul demanded.

This is why it is important not to hold tightly to traditional templates, be they robed choir plus organ or praise band or gospel choir. Another image of the Spirit—one that is linked closely to the creator Spirit—is that of the primordial, elementary Spirit: the force that supports all forces, or the life that grounds all life:

> Then the Lord God formed a man from the dust of the ground and breathed into his nostrils the breath of life, and the man became a living being.
>
> *Genesis 2:7*

Music that truly engages with the Spirit ought to feel that it's connecting us with something fundamental—within ourselves, within those around us and within the community that we serve. For some, traditional templates such as those mentioned above will help; for others, they will get in the way. A key role of the musical director is to discern how best to enable this connection for the *whole* community: both within the choir or music group *and* within the congregation. This means getting to know the musical talents and backgrounds that exist within *both* and allowing them to inspire and feed off each other.

Too often the relationship between musicians and congregation is treated as if it is one-way: that the musicians impart something to the congregation, which enables them to worship or reflect or praise more deeply. Of course this happens—and is very important—but it is not the end of the story. There is a key part of the relationship that flows from congregation to musicians, that has a role in shaping everything: from the musical configuration (choir or instrumental group or cantor etc.) to the repertoire and how it is approached. Keeping this part of the relationship active is essential, lest the music scene drifts and ceases to serve the worshipping community. It cannot be kept active if as musical directors we focus on the sound made by the existing arrangements, and fail to immerse ourselves in the community and get to know people.

In doing so, we might find that the same congregation-musician relationship that can open exciting avenues to explore is also rather constraining. The congregation might have sung only the well-known, "standard" hymns; or there might be groans at the thought of trying something "classical". The trick is to find repertoire that begins to move away from the norm, but that remains sufficiently close to it so as not to raise eyebrows (too far). Music from Taizé and Iona are particularly good at appealing across the range of musical traditions. If you are so inclined, it can be fun and very fulfilling to write your own music. It needn't be long and complicated; indeed, the beauty of the music of Taizé and Iona is its simplicity, yet its effectiveness. As Bach demonstrated, music written out of necessity can be both pragmatic and extraordinarily good.

In a letter to her friend Elisabeth of Schönau, the visionary St Hildegard of Bingen writes:

> Those who long to perfect the works of God . . . should leave heavenly things to him who is heavenly; for they are exiles, ignorant of the celestial, only singing the hiddenness of God, in the same way a trumpet only brings forth sounds but does not cause them: another must blow into it, for the sound to emerge. So too I, lying low in pusillanimity of fear, at times resound a little, like a small trumpet note from the living brightness.[47]

Hildegard's point is that she considers herself to be an instrument of God and that, consequently, her visions and her interpretation of them are divinely inspired. But there is also something striking in the way Hildegard describes her*self* as resounding like a trumpet note; not just her voice or the parts of her body that produce her voice, but her whole being: "*I* . . . at times resound a little, like a small trumpet note from the living brightness." Just as the whole of a trumpet is involved in producing trumpet notes, so the whole of you is involved in producing vocal notes: your physiology, of course, but also your cultural background, personality, hopes and fears, formative experiences, and so on. You cannot truly resound in song while consistently suppressing any one of these, any more than a trumpet can produce a convincing note with a chunk cut out of its tubing.

We have already seen how singers in a choir need to listen to and accommodate each other, and how this helps to instil the sort of behaviour towards others that Paul had in mind when building the body of Christ. However, this can tip over into something that suppresses individuality in favour of homogeneity. Training singers to blend with each other is an essential element of choir rehearsals, but can feel like an attempt to wring all distinctiveness from their voices, or even exclude certain voices from participating at all on the basis that they "aren't blend-able". Choir dress such as robes are a useful symbol of unity—of a body of individuals who are producing a single, coherent sound—but can feel like an attempt to hide the real person behind a screen.

This can be a symptom of a reasonable concern to avoid being distracted away from the intended subject of the music and towards the individuals who are delivering the music, or even the music itself.[48] However, this isn't about making individuals or glorious harmonies the object of worship, but using the diverse range of talents and experiences to produce music that touches all corners of the congregation. Music is incarnational in the sense that it offers a glimpse of a glorious, alternative reality through the actions of a human body: actions that are consequently shaped by the physical properties of that body as well as its journey through a particular culture and set of experiences. This is something that can be covered up and brushed aside, or something that can be acknowledged and used to make that glimpse a bit clearer.[49]

One cannot help but feel that, if Gareth Malone had tackled the early Christian community in Corinth, Paul would have smiled with favour upon him. In the BBC series *Unsung Town*, Malone was faced with the challenge of building a community choir in the unlikely context of South Oxhey. (Appropriately in the context of this book, the idea that sparked *Unsung Town* came from Canon Pam Wise, who was a vicar in South Oxhey at the time.) His approach was to get alongside those whom he would eventually entice into the choir; to find out what made them tick, and what made them sing. There is one amusing scene where, to the soundtrack of "The Sugar Plum Fairy", he goes one round in the boxing ring with "Matty", whom Malone describes as a "paler, smaller version of De Niro in *Raging Bull*".[50] Matty and Malone couldn't be more different. Having attracted a sizeable (200+) choir, he went back to the recruitment phase after realizing that it wasn't representative of the whole of South Oxhey. The result was a choir that broke down divisions, enabled musical gifts to flourish, and which helped the community to express and respond to deep-seated frustrations: that South Oxhey is invisible, forgotten and scorned by its opulent neighbours.[51]

Building a community choir from a town population of 12,000 with the benefit of TV cameras and the promise of an appearance on the BBC is different to building a church choir from a single congregation, but one cannot help but feel that Malone's approach gets a lot right when the aim is to build a community that embraces diversity, not just to make a beautiful sound.

Questions for discussion

Describe a time when you experienced music in worship that expressed what the gathered people were really trying to say, deep down. Discuss to what extent the musical provision in your worshipping community is able to achieve this.

Describe the diversity in your worshipping community, in all its forms. Then, discuss how that diversity might be expressed and celebrated by the community through music.

Describe the connections between those who provide the music (e.g. choir members, instrumentalists) and the rest of the worshipping community. Explore how these can be used to involve the *whole* of the community in worship.

4

Engaging those Beyond Your Worshipping Community

I started attending church at around the age of twelve. I had recently moved to secondary school and one of my newfound buddies was in a production of Andrew Lloyd Webber's *Joseph and the Amazing Technicolor Dreamcoat*, staged by a local Lutheran church. I went along and had a ball as the back end of a donkey. From there I started attending the youth club that was run by the church, and then the church itself. It didn't take long until the pastor and the elders discovered that I played the piano and offered to pay for organ lessons if I played once a month for services, to give the longstanding and elderly organist some respite. Proud to be asked to undertake such a responsibility, I didn't hesitate in agreeing.

The church in question was conservative; indeed, I didn't realize quite how conservative until a few years later when my eyes were opened to the vast range of views even within a single Christian denomination. I was often sceptical about what I heard from the pulpit and catechism classes, and asked the pastor questions such as "How can I be in heaven if I know that my loved ones are in eternal torment in hell?" I was rarely convinced by the answers I got back. Part of me (sometimes most of me) was rather pleased about this—evidence that I was cleverer than they—but it meant that I began to feel isolated in a sea of people who believed some rather strange things. To make matters worse, my friends at the church were becoming increasingly involved in the local American Football club. I joined in when we played in the school playground, but couldn't face the three-hour training sessions at the weekend. We were drifting apart. This, along with the pressure of exams at school, meant that I almost stopped coming to church, and probably would have stopped, if it wasn't for playing the organ.

It had really grabbed me. I got a real buzz from it. During the final verse of a particularly rousing hymn, I would open some particularly tasty stops in the swell— definitely a "mixture", sometimes a "reed"—and close the swell box, reducing the volume so you could just about sense they were there, building in the background. Then, at an opportune moment I would open the swell box and unleash the extra oomph and pizazz, and the congregation would sing their heart out. That was a real thrill.

My role as occasional organist also meant that I got to chat to a much broader range of people than my teenage friends, and about a much broader range of things than

American Football, girls and TV. Through my organ teacher, I was asked to play in a variety of churches to fill gaps, which started to expose me to the diversity of beliefs and worship styles. I found this fascinating, prompting further vigorous conversations with the pastor.

After university I returned home, worked two jobs concurrently and used the money I saved to backpack around Australia for six months. I shall never forget the pastor praying on the Sunday before I flew to Brisbane that "fleets of angels" accompany me on my travels. If it wasn't for an innate scepticism about all things that don't conform to the laws of nature, I might have believed that his prayer was answered. For my journey across Australia was defined by church, even though I didn't plan it that way. On arriving at a city, I would rock up to the local Lutheran church, offer my services as an organist, and find myself becoming part of that community for a few weeks, even living with members of the congregation who kindly offered me hospitality. I'm sure they were more interested in—and made curious by—the rare sighting of an English Lutheran, but music gave me a route into the community and the role and purpose I needed to feel a functioning, contributing part of it.

Although lasting only six months, this trip was a formative part of my life. I returned from it slightly more relaxed in my own skin and with a clearer idea of what I wanted to do next. While I was travelling, church music was right at the heart of this subtle but fundamental transformation, acting like a sort of catalyst, much as it had done during my teens.

The same happened when I moved to Sheffield to pursue postgraduate studies in philosophy and was hooked into the Anglican church of St Mark's, Broomhill by some fellow students. I was happy enough for the first year or so, playing the piano for all-age services and hanging out in the Broomhill Tavern, but it wasn't until I became musical director and engaged more deeply in the community that I really felt this transformation process kick in again, and realized how much I had missed it.

Joining a church choir as a sort of baptism

Three of the major themes of Paul's understanding of baptism are illustrated by the following passages:[52]

> For we were all baptized by [or 'in' or 'with'] one Spirit so as to form one body—whether Jews or Gentiles, slave or free—and we were all given the one Spirit to drink.
>
> *1 Corinthians 12:13*

> So in Christ Jesus you are all children of God through faith, for all of you who were baptized into Christ have clothed yourselves with Christ. There is neither

> Jew nor Gentile, neither slave nor free, nor is there
> male and female, for you are all one in Christ Jesus.
>
> *Galatians 3:26–28*

Firstly, as both passages suggest, Paul considers baptism to be the incorporation rite into the body of Christ. Secondly, Paul considers baptism to confer upon the individual a transformed identity, which is rendered in the passage from Galatians as the individual "clothing themselves with Christ". There is also the sense, in both passages, that social, racial and even gender differences between individuals have been abolished within the body of Christ, as if the new identity supersedes them all, and puts everyone on an equal footing. Thirdly, there is the sense that the individual is empowered through baptism. The passage from Corinthians connects baptism with the Spirit, and it is the Spirit, for Paul, that enables individuals to grow and nurture their faith, not least through conferring spiritual gifts.[53]

These three themes, which Paul considers to be fundamental features of baptism, are also characteristic of joining a church choir (or undertaking a range of musical roles in church)—including a choir that is nascent and developing. Your identity is transformed in the sense that you assume a role and function within the worshipping community: you are now a choir member. Some churches even offer a quick ceremony as part of worship to induct new members into the choir, perhaps after a period of training. And although this isn't an "official" incorporation rite into the body of Christ, it certainly makes you feel that you belong—that you're a functioning part of it, rather than just along for the ride. This belonging can be key, particularly if you've started to drift away because, like me, you begin to doubt what you hear from the pulpit, or you drift apart from the people who attracted you there in the first place. Finally, becoming part of the choir empowers you and enables you to grow spiritually. We have already seen how singing in a church choir enables you to "engage with the Spirit". Furthermore, by singing parts of the liturgy you inevitably learn more about it. You are automatically put into contact with a range of people, who themselves can be an essential source of spiritual nourishment and growth. Social, racial and gender divides are removed or at least made insignificant, just as in Paul's vision of the baptized body of Christ: music can be a great leveller.[54]

A transformed self-identity; a sense of belonging; and spiritual growth. All three themes feature in what Andy wrote when I asked him to reflect on his experience of joining St John's Choir, shortly after arriving at the church. Andy—a self-effacing, shy man who took some persuasion to join the choir—was rediscovering Christianity at the time:

> I could've denied it all [the fact he could sing] and sat
> there on my tod every Sunday. But how much richer
> has my whole church, worship and companionship
> experience been for the spirituality of our music. . . .

> I feel so much more part of St John's because I was
> asked to sing. They had the confidence I didn't. But
> now I do have it and I carry it in everything I do both
> in church and outside.

So, joining a church choir can feel very much like being baptized into the body of Christ. It is also a very effective baptism. Perseverance and discipline are required after baptism to maintain the lifelong process of growing spiritually. Being a member of a choir focuses the task, almost into bite-sized chunks, and makes it concrete— you are learning these pieces for this particular worship service—and provides you with a micro-community of people with the same task, who support each other to achieve it. This might just make the task less daunting and more manageable.[55]

Just as there is a journey that the individual goes through, where the incorporation rite is somewhere near the beginning, so there is a journey that the choir itself goes through, that begins with individuals turning up to perform a function, and which ends up with something much deeper. I had an inkling that this was beginning to happen when people started to describe themselves in terms of being a member of the choir—when it became part of their self-identity—and when I realized that the choir was developing an ethos of its own. "Ethos" is difficult to pin down, but I find it helpful to think of it in terms of load-bearing bricks: the ones that, if removed, lead to the wall tumbling down, like in a game of Jenga. Inclusivity was (and still is) a load-bearing brick of St John's Choir: one that, if removed to improve the quality of sound, would have fundamentally changed the choir into something very different. In contrast, singing classical pieces, whilst very useful in maintaining a varied repertoire, constituted one of those bricks that I hoped to keep, but if removed would have left the structure intact.

Working on the boundary between the body of Christ and wider society

Baptism marks one of the boundaries between the body of Christ and wider society. As new people are incorporated into the body and visitors turn up to the ritual itself, it is where the unity that is the body of Christ is thrown open and expanded. In the baptism service—and in other services where there are guests, such as weddings and funerals—the church musician needs to find a way of working somewhere on that boundary, such that the music is appropriate for the worship and the context of the particular worshipping community, but also speaks to those who consider themselves outside or on the fringe of that community, and indeed the body of Christ.

This is important, because music is a key tool in expressing Christianity, as reflected in a range of literature. For example, in Messiaen's opera *St Francois d'Assise*, St Francis asks an angel if he might be given a foretaste of heaven. The angel responds with a paraphrase of Thomas Aquinas: "God dazzles us by an excess of truth; music transports us to God by an absence of truth."[56] In other words, propositional language can only express so much when it comes to the nature of God; music is an additional tool that enables you to express more. Similarly, Elisabeth-Paule Labat, gripped by the experience of hearing a violinist play Mozart's *Sonata in E Minor*, was inspired to argue that music is a language, but a language of signs and not propositions: signs that point towards a "greater beauty" and ultimately towards God.[57] It is because music functions differently to propositional language that it is able to "express the ineffable".[58] For instance, because it is not linear in the same way as propositional language, it is able to express opposing themes at the same time,[59] and "can even unite them in harmonisation and counterpoint".[60]

It is tempting to think of the boundary between the body of Christ and wider society as a clear line. However, like the boundary between land and sea, it might appear that way from a distance, but upon closer examination you find that matters aren't so simple, and that there are narrow peninsulas and underground estuaries and all manner of ways in which land and sea are entwined. Well-known church repertoire is peppered with examples of the sacred and secular overlapping, such as hymn tunes that started life as secular songs (e.g. Sydney Carter's "Lord of the Dance", set to the tune of a Shaker

song: "Simple Gifts"); and, as Lucy Winkett argues in
Our Sound is Our Wound, "Scriptural cadences" can be
discerned in "secular" popular and classical music, such
as lyrics from Ms Dynamite's album *Judgement Days*
that are reminiscent of Christ dividing the sheep from
the goats in Matthew 25:31–46.[61]

The challenge for the church musician is to find
those points of overlap that are appropriate for their
community. For example, in the year 1746, Charles
Wesley was preaching in Plymouth. He was forced to
stop when a rowdy group of off-duty sailors launched
into a fruity version of a popular song. His reaction was
to invite everyone back that evening. He spent the rest
of the day writing alternative lyrics to the same tune and
returned that evening to lead the crowd in song, but this
time singing his words.[62]

Wesley showed how, by thinking beyond traditional
repertoire and meeting the audience where they are
at, you can engage individuals who wouldn't normally
engage with Christianity. He found the boundary and
successfully navigated his way to one of those points of
overlap.

In building a choir from scratch, you often find
yourself with something that naturally exists closer to
that boundary. For one thing, although a few might
have previous experience, overall you are unlikely to
have a group of people who are steeped in a particular
"churchy" repertoire, be it classical or otherwise. This
can be a blessing, particularly if you are seeking

suggestions for a forthcoming baptism or wedding, or if you intend to ask the choir to sing something a bit beyond the norm. They are more likely to be able to think and sing "outside of the box".

Furthermore, in building a choir from scratch, it is not a given that the worshipping community would be able to afford, or even want, choir dress, such as robes. There are various reasons why choir dress of some sort is effective: for instance, returning to the idea that joining a choir can feel like a baptism into the body of Christ, the wearing of robes or other symbols can make this feel real, as if you are "clothing yourself with Christ". However, a downside, particularly with very obvious dress such as robes, is that it takes the choir a little further from that boundary. In February 2017, John Bercow, Speaker of the House of Commons, announced that clerks will no longer wear wigs so to "convey to the public a marginally less stuffy and forbidding image of this chamber at work".[63] Similarly, not having robes or suchlike can be a blessing.

The deeper point here is that church music isn't always about producing something that is set apart from the everyday; it is often about looking at the everyday differently and seeing how it points to something beyond; something greater. In a nascent, developing choir you have just that, happening right before your eyes: something that has taken the everyday and is beginning to transform it and the community of which it is part into something more Christlike. It is almost as if you have two realities juxtaposed. The first is the one you know: the people in the choir, who you can still hear, voice by voice, and see; people you know to varying degrees, including their strengths, faults and idiosyncrasies. The second one is the emerging reality: the sound of diverse voices in harmony, where you are on that boundary of still being able to pick out the individual voices, but they are listening for each other, adjusting, accommodating, and producing this extraordinary sound. You have the raw materials, the process by which they are being moulded to be more Christlike, and the beginnings of the fruits of that process. And, to anyone observing it over time, that gives you an immediate sense of what is possible not just for them but also for you—all the more so because you already, to an extent, identify with them, and they identify with you.

Questions for discussion

Discuss to what extent the musical provision in your worshipping community welcomes and nurtures (i) those who are new to your community; (ii) those who are new to the Christian faith.

Describe the journey of your choir or music group, if possible since inception. What are the load-bearing bricks that, if removed, would fundamentally change your choir or music group into something different?

Describe occasions when the musical provision in your worshipping community has successfully "worked on the boundary" between the body of Christ and wider society. Explore ways in which this could happen more often, and more effectively.

5

Implications for Church Music Today

In sum, leading and developing music in the context of worship, such as by creating a choir that is drawn from the congregation, is incredibly important, because it is an effective way of building Christlike communities, which is a fundamental purpose of any Christian congregation. We have explored its effectiveness using Paul's metaphor of the "body of Christ" and his vision of how the body is formed and then built up.

Firstly, individuals are united by the Spirit. We have seen how singing together enables an engagement with the Spirit in several ways. It requires you to listen to and accommodate others, which provides an ongoing discipline that nudges your behaviour, attitude and outlook towards something more Christlike. This is what Paul referred to as "walking with the Spirit". The experience of singing in harmony—even straightforward harmony that is widely achievable—gives you a visceral sense of an alternative reality, which is also a feature of other experiences that are "of the Spirit", such as in the Pentecostal and Charismatic movements. This alternative reality is the sort of community Paul envisaged: one where all are united into a whole that is greater than the sum of its parts, but where individuality is maintained and diverse gifts are celebrated. Similarly to Spirit-led worship, this often involves the unexpected and invites spontaneity, which can open the door to the glorious.

The second stage is for the body to be built up and invigorated. Paul was clear on how this is achieved: for him, "love builds up" and that means acting as Christ did. Looking within the worshipping community, an example of the sort of behaviour Paul had in mind is what he termed "discerning the body of Christ", which means involving everyone, in all their diversity, in worship. We explored how building the musical provision from the congregation is particularly effective in achieving this. Music can help a group to respond to and begin to process significant events, such as the death of a much-loved member of the community. This is enhanced when, for instance, a choir is drawn from the congregation, because the line between the two is especially blurred. Hopefully, the diversity within the congregation is reflected in or understood by members of the choir, which provides an invaluable resource to celebrate it, such as by sparking repertoire choices. If the choir (or other musical provision) is built from scratch, there is an opportunity to build it around the needs and talents of the individuals within the congregation, which will naturally draw out some of that diversity.

Looking beyond the worshipping community, we saw how joining a church choir (or instrumental group), including a nascent, developing one, can feel very much like a baptism into the body of Christ. This is because, like Paul's understanding of baptism as an incorporation rite into the body, the discipline of singing with the choir involves a transformed personal identity, empowerment through the Spirit and the breaking down of social, racial and gender barriers. We also explored how a new choir can exist nearer to the boundary between the body of Christ and wider society, and therefore can be an effective way of engaging those on the fringes or outside of the body of Christ.

Putting it into practice

So, what does this mean for me? Firstly, if you lead music in worship, you should hold your head high, whether you are accompanying hymns on the piano for a congregation of fifteen, persevering with a choir of eight or leading a large, thriving choir or high-end instrumental group. For you are in the business of helping to transform people and communities into the body of Christ. It might not feel like it when you're ten minutes into the rehearsal and half the choir are yet to turn up, or you look across from the piano stool at the dwindling congregation of fifteen. But you are enabling people to sing together and therefore to listen to and accommodate each other in ways that might just seep into their everyday interactions with others. You are bringing another language into worship that helps the community to engage, reflect and express themselves in ways they couldn't otherwise, and that helps them to see how the world could be. You are providing a way in which those who are new to the community can deepen their understanding of Christianity and truly feel that they belong.

The second implication is that, often, you don't have to do much to get this transformative process going. Small steps make a big difference, such as the gradual introduction of some short, straightforward chants, songs or rounds; or, more ambitiously, the forming of an occasional singing or instrumental group to help lead the congregation. Of course, this needs someone to take the initiative and step up, and my aim in this book is to highlight the benefits of doing so that often go unnoticed and under-appreciated. I'm hoping that this will help to persuade someone to act on that niggle that they can make a difference.

The third implication is a challenge. You may already be a music leader and more than happy with your lot because, every Sunday, you are at the helm of a large, fine choir; or because you accompany a small congregation who are openly very appreciative of what you do, from which you (rightly) gain much satisfaction. Are you doing all you can to help transform the whole, diverse worshipping community in your midst?

What could I be doing? This will depend on your skills, experience and time, and on the circumstances of your worshipping community. However, I cannot see how any music leader can build Christlike communities effectively without engaging with the congregation in a sustained and meaningful way. Therefore, I would encourage you to:

1. **Reach out.** If you haven't already, get to know the people in the congregation, new and not-so-new, focusing on their background, culture, hopes, fears and personalities *first* and only then their musical skills and experience. Get to know the ministers and their vision for the community.

2. **Draw out.** Use what you've learned to (1) pick appropriate repertoire that draws out and celebrates the diversity within the congregation; and (2) identify opportunities to encourage people to offer their voices and instruments in worship.

3. **Work out.** Introduce simple music that requires people to really listen to and accommodate each other, such as short songs in straightforward harmony, rounds, and chants that are sung in "free time" as if you are speaking them (e.g. Gregorian chants).[64] Rehearse with the congregation regularly and develop a discipline.

4. **Look out.** Look for the opportunities that are created when things don't go to plan. Be suspicious when it's feeling routine, straightforward and rather comfortable.

5. **Sing out!** Have confidence in the importance of what you're doing. Focus on the good you and those you lead are generating rather than the musical challenges you are working through.

By way of illustration, here is one journey that broadly reflects what I've seen happen in a number of communities, of different Christian denominations, with few musical resources:

1. Unless you have relevant training already and feel confident about finding and then teaching appropriate, simple-but-effective repertoire, get yourself on a course, such as the RSCM's *Lift Up Your Voice*. Go and see how it is done in other worshipping communities with a tradition similar to or compatible with your own.

2. Talk to your minister(s) and congregation and find a pastoral or thematic reason to try something different. It could be a significant day in the cultural calendar of the congregation or an ethnic group within it; or a service that focuses on climate change.

3. Find one or two relevant chants, rounds or short songs written in straightforward harmony. Make

sure that they don't depart too far from the style of music to which the congregation is accustomed. Find a time to practise them with the congregation prior to the target service—before, during or after the main Sunday service is ideal when you have a captive audience.

4. When you introduce them into worship, don't worry if they are sung less than perfectly. You've already taken a significant step forward. Ride the momentum: suggest that the congregation turns this into a regular discipline and practises once a month.

5. You might find that some enjoy this new initiative more than others. Ask those who are clearly in the former camp if they would like to do this more often and perhaps try something more ambitious. See if you can't get a small singing group together.

6. If you do manage to form a group, you may find that some people are unreliable, that you never get the whole group for any rehearsal, and that the music doesn't sound how you hoped it would. You will naturally seek ways to remedy this, but it is important to put it in context and make peace with it. If you've got this far, you've taken a quantum leap from where you were. Find someone to talk to who will help you develop this perspective.

7. Whether or not you form a singing group, make sure you keep rehearsing with the congregation. Keep looking for different ways to engage people.

If you conduct a choir, try turning around and conducting the congregation. If the choir is behind everyone in the balcony or hidden behind a rood screen, try re-locating them near the congregation occasionally so that you (and they) can engage with the congregation. Encourage someone who plays an instrument to accompany a hymn; or accompany *them* while they offer a voluntary. Get someone to teach you about church music that is relevant to them—such as from their cultural background, or a different Christian tradition—and, if possible, find a way of incorporating it into worship. Generate a culture of openness, participation and inclusion.

Adopting any of the above principles, in one way or another, will be a significant departure from the norm for many music leaders. It may not be something to which they are well suited: being a good accompanist on organ or piano does not mean that they have the interpersonal skills to encourage the congregation into the musical life of the church; or that they are able to teach harmony to a group of non-sight-readers. Where this cannot be fixed via training, it might be sensible to seek someone with a complementary skillset to augment the existing music leader. To support communities who would find it hard to identify such a person, I would encourage a more active sharing of resources, including across denominations. Too often we find several congregations who struggle to find an accompanist Sunday by Sunday within a mile of a church where there are two organists, several pianists and a number of people who could teach a short chant competently. Sometimes people just need to be asked, perhaps by their minister, to lend an occasional hand where they could make a significant difference.

It may be felt that this approach will not work in all contexts: particularly, churches where the music is dispatched from the front by a high-quality choir or worship band. Choral Evensong in a cathedral would be a clear example, as would many other churches where the congregation expects to sing the hymns or worship songs but leaves anything else to the musicians "up front".

I accept that there are certain services, such as Choral Evensong, where introducing more congregational participation would turn them into something very different and perhaps defeat the objective.[65] However, beyond distinctive services such as Evensong, there will be other services where it is much easier to think creatively and involve the congregation more in the music-making. Indeed, an excellent choir or instrumental group, used appropriately, can really support a congregation in learning new music (e.g. by singing or playing a new chant so the congregation can hear it before attempting it) and singing a round or harmony (e.g. by dispersing the choir or instruments into the congregation to reinforce the vocal lines).

Introducing this into a community that is not used to it will inevitably bring challenges, but the benefits of doing so are high enough, I would argue, to merit giving it a go.

It may be felt that I am arguing for a relaxation of musical standards; that it's acceptable to allow the sort of poor musical provision within worship that distracts in the name of inclusion and building community.

On the contrary, it is through the discipline of rehearsing and trying, repeatedly, to listen more closely to and accommodate others, that the transformative process really gets going. We should avoid taking this to an extreme when the aim is to widen participation. There will be rough edges but, as I argued earlier, they can be profoundly meaningful in their own way. The trick is to find music that is within reach of most of the congregation and that can be worked up to a good standard, and then to teach it patiently and positively.

Whatever approach we want our music leaders to take needs to be reflected in their training and by those who support and oversee them. For me, that approach needs to be one that best enables the transformative power of music-making, and I would like to see more attention given to the role of music leaders in transforming individuals and communities. It also needs to be clear in job adverts, but I am struck by the tendency of many of these, particularly in high-resource contexts, to de-prioritize certain non-musical but important aspects of the role, such as marking as "desirable but non-essential" a willingness to "become a member of the church community". Unless you immerse yourself in the community you serve, you will miss opportunities to build the body of Christ.

There is a much deeper problem that is revealed by job adverts (or, more precisely, the lack of them): one that takes us back to the beginning of this book and the main motivation behind it. The roles that are advertised tend to be the ones that offer something by way of a salary, an impressive choir or instrumental group to direct, or a fine organ that has been refurbished recently. Many vacancies in low-resource contexts are not advertised, possibly because there is little confidence that anyone would apply, or because filling them is not considered to be important enough. There is a real danger that music in these communities slips away and we lose a fundamental and effective tool that helps us build the body of Christ. Remedying this situation must begin by changing mindsets; by convincing musicians and the communities they serve of the importance of what they do, in high- *and* low-resource contexts. I hope, in a small way, to have contributed towards this.

When we can't gather

As I write this, a significant proportion of the world population is slowly emerging from lockdown following the COVID-19 pandemic. Public worship is resuming, albeit with significant limitations, not least on the use of music.

Congregations have been unable to gather—at least as they normally do. Many have found ways of meeting virtually and keeping in touch via social media. Some churches have streamed their worship services, often with viewing figures that have been much higher than expected. Some who don't use the internet have received pastoral phone calls.

Although unusual for many, the inability to gather is normal for a vast range of Christians across the globe. The reasons are various: disability; persecution; illness; natural disasters; unreconciled differences, to name but a few. We have all received a limited sense of what this is like but, for many of us, we have been lucky enough to endure the restrictions in the knowledge that they will come to an end and we will be able to gather again.

The body of Christ has felt very different throughout lockdown. As I outlined in Chapter 1, the body, as Paul envisaged it, consists of the people and not the buildings, or even the ritual activities that happen in those buildings. However, Christianity's association with a distinctive kind of building—a church—is part of its identity for many people. Consequently, whilst those buildings have been off-limits, it has felt to many as though part of that identity has been lost.

Without buildings and public rituals to distinguish (or distract?) us, we as Christians have had no alternative but to *be* the body of Christ: to act it out in our everyday lives. COVID-19 has refocused us on caring for each other. Making sure that the vulnerable in our community have what they need. Befriending someone who is isolated and needs a chat. Amid the suffering and challenges brought by COVID-19, this has been a useful and healthy reorientation. It is closer to the whole-life-encompassing, Pauline concept of worship that I described in Chapter 1. It brings the body closer to what Paul had in mind: one that is less concerned with bricks and mortar and the "right" way of conducting rituals, and more concerned with those in need.

Even under lockdown, we have continued to make music to bind, invigorate and grow our communities, which is a testament to its versatility and the importance we afford it to this end. I have been particularly struck by the virtual choirs and instrumental groups that have invited everyone and anyone to record themselves against a well-known hymn or song, and then spliced the recordings into a mass choir or orchestra.[66] It has been a great way of sustaining participation whilst we can't gather. It has also retained many of the transformative elements of live music-making. The process of creating the recordings still required individuals to submit to a common tempo and sing/play in a way that is respectful of the fact that they will be joined with others. The final product still reflected a powerful image of an alternative reality—of a community of diverse individuals joined in harmony. Indeed, for those virtual groups that have presented their musicians as a tapestry of thumbnail-sized videos, there has been something extra powerful about seeing people in their own homes, in their slacks, singing or playing away as one. A potent sense of individuality retained in community.

These projects are also a good example of how, by thinking creatively, we can reach out to and involve individuals whom we may not otherwise reach. The communities that have been created through virtual choirs and instrumental groups have looked very different to the communities that gather in the churches that have organized them. Refreshingly different. They have included people that we would never expect to see or hear, on a Sunday morning, helping to lead the music. People who don't normally go to church. People who live on the other side of the globe, in cultures and political contexts that are very different to our own. Yet, all have been joined and engaged in solidarity, equally and inclusively.

It seems likely that many communities will want to capitalize on the success of virtual choirs, streamed services and other forms of internet-based outreach and continue (or even expand) their online provision long-term. As places of worship re-open, some might decide, at least temporarily, to offer additional services to fit everyone in, because social distancing will reduce significantly the maximum size of the congregation. There will be a need to continue streaming services to reach vulnerable individuals who cannot yet return to church.

More services; more online worship: this means a greater need for church musicians, at a time when many are facing an uncertain future. During the lockdown period, and in line with many lay staff across the Christian churches in the UK, most church musicians have been "furloughed"[67] (if paid) or simply unable to do what they do as volunteers. Some have been made redundant. The wellbeing of church musicians in this context is an obvious and key issue, as with many others across the world who have faced significant disruption and a drop in income. A recent discussion hosted by RSCM on the future of music ministry following COVID-19 highlighted the danger that church musicians lose confidence in themselves and the importance of what they do.[68] The need to reassure church musicians that they provide a vital service to the church—a key message of this book—is greater than ever.

COVID-19 has brought hardship for many, not least those who have lost loved ones or have been seriously ill. As we begin to gather again, I hope it will be with a keener sensitivity to the needs of those around us, and for the potential of music-making, done creatively, to reach out and transform us into the body of Christ.

Questions for discussion

How might your community use music to support online outreach? Ideas might include virtual choirs or instrumental groups, or providing music for streamed worship.

Thinking back to your answers to the questions throughout this book, what changes do you need to make to ensure the musical provision in your worshipping community builds the body of Christ most effectively?

Identify any changes that can be made quickly and easily. For those that require a bit more thought and resource, work out a plan to make them happen.

If there are musical leadership roles that need filling in your community, draft a notional job advert for one that makes clear what skills, qualities and experience are needed. Think of how to attract potential candidates by highlighting the difference they could make and positive experiences they could have.

Postlude

It's the day of the choir commissioning service, when St John's Choir will be officially incorporated into the structures of the church. This was Giles' idea—one he suggested to me when I was hitting a low point and struggling to keep the momentum going. The aim is to affirm and celebrate how far the choir has come since inception, eighteen months ago.

I read through the text of the commissioning ceremony. It describes music as a *ministry*. I pause on that word. For years it's all been rather simple for me: the church musician delivers the music. End of story. But that's not how it's described here. The text mentions musical talent, but otherwise the focus is on serving the worshipping community: on promoting "unity, peace and love in the church and in the world, and especially among those with whom you lead worship".

Against that set of standards, I feel rather pleased with how we've started. New and not-so-new have found a home in the choir. It is a genuinely open, cheerful, welcoming group. The diversity within the congregation is largely reflected in the choir: eight different nationalities; a range of ages and musical abilities; the wealthy and not-so-wealthy. Most people in the congregation should be able to identify with someone in the choir, making it an accessible and visible symbol of unity.

We have developed musically, too, which is impacting the worship. The congregational singing has lifted. Choir pieces are sounding more confident. For the first time in living memory, rather than the normal hum of chitter-chatter, there is genuine, prayerful silence at the end of Communion after the choir piece finishes.

People talk about the choir and how things have changed. Where there was resignation, there's now a buzz.

The choir standing in front of me, ready to begin the pre-service rehearsal, feels huge. I count twenty-five. The two key pieces are "Over my Head", which we will sing as an introit from the balcony, and "Exsultate Justi": a joyful, exuberant piece by John Williams, composed as part of his soundtrack to Steven Spielberg's movie *Empire of the Sun*.

I feel confident about "Over my Head". Learning from previous mistakes, during the Monday rehearsals I really hammered the sustained "hmm-ing" notes that accompany the solo and made sure that the response line "There is music in the air" will be delivered confidently and emphatically.

I'm more nervous about "Exsultate". It wasn't a great choice, with hindsight. I underestimated how difficult it would be for the non-sight-readers to learn their parts, which are long and entirely in Latin. I also failed to spot a very high, top A for the sopranos in the penultimate bar and again in the final chord. During rehearsals, one or two could reach it; one or two really couldn't (but tried anyway); the rest just gave up. This meant that the piece climaxed with a rather thin-sounding discord, rather than the bright, full-bodied major chord that was written.

Fortunately, the choir has taken it upon themselves to rise to the occasion. I issued recordings of all the parts and people have clearly done their homework. There have even been extra rehearsals organized by choir members in their own homes. We battled through the Latin, the notes and the rhythm until they came good. I found a diplomatic way of suggesting that only those sopranos who can manage it take the top A; the others sing the same note an octave lower. We grafted until, in the final rehearsal, we sang the piece all the way through without it falling apart. They must have heard the cheers in Waterloo Station.

After the pre-service run-through we take our seats in the balcony, waiting for the service to begin.

At 10.30 a.m. Giles enters from the vestry and asks the congregation to stand. I give the choir their notes from the organ, scoot across to my music stand and we launch into "Over my Head".

For the first time, St John's Choir fills the sonic space in that large, cavernous church, the balcony funnelling the sound outwards like a megaphone. By the end of the first bar, I am bursting with pride.

That sets the tone for the rest of the service. "Exsultate" is robust and a little rough around the edges—the sopranos' top A certainly tests the windows—but full of spirit and confidence. Even the hymns are sung, by all, with gusto.

For the commissioning itself, the choir lines up in front of the altar. They seem surprised to be there. After the responses, Giles vests each of them with the new choir dress, designed by the choir: a golden scarf, embroidered with the red St John's cross. They look fantastic.

The commissioning ends with a prayer and a blessing.

> May the Lord give you wisdom, imagination, courage, strength and love to lead and make music to God's praise and glory.
>
> And the blessing of God Almighty, Creator, Redeemer and Sustainer, rest upon you, and on your work done in God's name, now and always.
>
> Amen.

Bibliography

Arnold, Jonathan, *Sacred Music in Secular Society* (Farnham: Ashgate, 2014).

Archbishops' Commission on Church Music, *In Tune with Heaven* (London: Church House Publishing, 1992).

Begbie, Jeremy, *Theology, Music and Time* (Cambridge: Cambridge University Press, 2000).

Begbie, Jeremy, *Resounding Truth* (Grand Rapids, MI: Baker Academic, 2007).

Begbie, Jeremy, "Faithful Feelings", in Begbie, Jeremy and Guthrie, Steven (eds) *Resonant Witness* (Grand Rapids, MI: Eerdmans, 2011).

Bell, John, *The Singing Thing Too* (Glasgow: Wild Goose, 2007).

Brewer, Mike, *Mike Brewer's Warm-Ups!* (London: Faber, 2002).

Day, Thomas, *Why Catholics Can't Sing* (New York: Crossroad, 2002).

Epstein, Heidi, *Melting the Venusberg: A Feminist Theology of Music* (New York: Continuum, 2004).

Fee, Gordon, *The First Epistle to the Corinthians* (Grand Rapids, MI: Eerdmans, 1987).

Fee, Gordon, *Paul, the Spirit, and the People of God* (Grand Rapids, MI: Baker Academic, 2011).

Gooder, Paula, *Body* (London: SPCK, 2016).

Guthrie, Steven, "The Wisdom of Song" in Begbie, Jeremy and Guthrie, Steven (eds) *Resonant Witness* (Grand Rapids, MI: Eerdmans, 2011).

Horn, Stacy, *Imperfect Harmony* (Chapel Hill, NC: Algonquin, 2013).

John, Jeffrey, *Permanent, Faithful, Stable* (London: Darton, Longman and Todd, 2007).

Karkkainen, Veli-Matti, *Pneumatology* (Grand Rapids, MI: Baker Academic, 2002).

Lee, Michelle V., *Paul, the Stoics, and the Body of Christ* (Cambridge: Cambridge University Press, 2008).

Malone, Gareth, *Choir* (London: Collins, 2013).

Meeks, Wayne, *The First Urban Christians* (New Haven: Yale University Press, 2003).

McGann, Mary, *Exploring Music as Worship and Theology* (Collegeville, MN: Liturgical Press, 2002).

Peterson, Dan, *Engaging with God* (Leicester: Apollos, 2002).

Rees, Robin, *Weary and Ill at Ease* (Leominster: Gracewing, 1993).

Routley, Erik, *Church Music and the Christian Faith* (Chicago, IL: Agape, 1978).

Saliers, Don E., *Music and Theology* (Nashville, TN: Abingdon Press, 2007).

Spong, John S., *Re-Claiming the Bible for a Non-Religious World* (New York: HarperCollins, 2013).

Taylor, John V., *The Go-Between God* (London: SCM Press, 1989).

Taylor, Nicholas, *Paul on Baptism* (London: SCM Press, 2016).

Tomlin, Graham, "Life in the Spirit", in Williams, Jane (ed.), *The Holy Spirit in the World Today* (London: Alpha, 2011).

Troeger, Thomas H., *Music as Prayer* (Oxford: Oxford University Press, 2013).

Varden, Erik, "Translator's Preface" to Labat, Elisabeth-Paule, (2014) *The Song That I Am* (Collegeville, MN: Liturgical Press, 2014).

Williams, Rowan, "The Holy Spirit in the Bible", in Williams, Jane (ed.), *The Holy Spirit in the World Today* (London: Alpha, 2011).

Winkett, Lucy, *Our Sound is our Wound* (London: Continuum, 2010).

Wren, Brian, *Praying Twice* (Louisville, KY: Westminster John Knox, 2000).

Wright, N. T., *The Epistle of Paul to the Colossians and to Philemon* (Grand Rapids, MI: Eerdmans, 1988).

Notes

1   See, for example, John Bell, *The Singing Thing Too* and Mike Brewer's *Warm-Ups* for sound, practical guidance on leading a choir; and the RSCM's *Sunday by Sunday* series for advice on hymn/song and choir repertoire choices.

2   Paul seems to say some things about women and about same-sex relationships that have been—and still are—extremely divisive. However, there is dispute over whether Paul wrote 1 Timothy, which contains one of the two key "anti-women" texts ("I do not permit a woman to teach or to assume authority over a man; she must be quiet" (1 Timothy 2:12)). The second appears in 1 Corinthians 14:34 and states that women "should remain silent in the churches", but appears to contradict an earlier verse suggesting that women can prophesy, leading some to suggest that it must have been added at a later date and not written by Paul. On same-sex relationships, a useful discussion of the complexities of reading Paul is offered by Jeffrey John in *Permanent, Faithful, Stable* (London: Darton, Longman and Todd, 2007), pp. 13ff.

3   Many Taizé chants are free to download on their website: <http://www.taize.fr/en>. For a list of Iona songbooks, see <https://www.ionabooks.com>.

4   See Dan Peterson, *Engaging with God* (Leicester: Apollos, 2002), pp. 177–9 and Archbishops' Commission on Church Music, *In*

Tune with Heaven (London: Church House Publishing, 1992), p. 39.

5 Paula Gooder, *Body* (London: SPCK, 2016), p. 119. See also Peterson, *Engaging with God*, pp. 153ff.

6 N. T. Wright, *The Epistle of Paul to the Colossians and to Philemon* (Grand Rapids, MI: Eerdmans, 1988), p. 176.

7 The notion that formal Christian gatherings are a practical expression of koinonia is suggested by Peterson, *Engaging with God*, p. 155.

8 Cf. Jonathan Arnold, *Sacred Music in Secular Society* (Farnham: Ashgate, 2014), who argues that " . . . there can be no divide between the church and the concert hall, or between religious and secular society, for the art of music is received by everyone alike" (p. 147). Arnold's argument is that sacred music enables individuals to contemplate themes such as suffering, loneliness, joy, peace or anger, and to explore "the indefinable, the inexpressible, that unknown to us and yet that for which we search and long" *whether or not* it is performed in church or the concert hall. My point is that there is an important difference in the expected response to music when delivered in a church rather than concert setting, in that the former is meant to facilitate the building of an active, Christlike community.

9 See Michelle V. Lee, *Paul, the Stoics, and the Body of Christ* (Cambridge: Cambridge University Press, 2008), pp. 129ff; 153.

10 For a brief description of the competing views, see Gordon Fee, *The First Epistle to the Corinthians* (Grand Rapids, MI: Eerdmans, 1987), pp. 604–5.

11 See Lee, *Paul, the Stoics, and the Body of Christ*, pp. 132–3. Another passage in which Paul draws a connection between

individuals and the Spirit, in virtue of which they are knitted together, is Romans 8:14–16: " . . . those who are led by the Spirit of God are the children of God. The Spirit you received does not make you slaves, so that you live in fear again; rather, the Spirit you received brought about your adoption to sonship. And by him we cry, 'Abba, Father'. The Spirit himself testifies with our spirit that we are God's children."

12 See Fee, *The First Epistle to the Corinthians*, p. 628; Lee, *Paul, the Stoics, and the Body of Christ*, p. 179.

13 See Lee, *Paul, the Stoics, and the Body of Christ*, pp. 194–5.

14 See, for example, Brian Wren, *Praying Twice* (Louisville: Westminster John Knox, 2000), who opens his sub-section "Clergy and Musicians" with " . . . relationships between clergy and musicians are not always marked by understanding and respect" (pp. 140–1). See also *In Tune with Heaven,* which reports a "widespread impression that breakdowns in the relationship between clergy and musicians are common" (p. 190).

15 Robin Rees, *Weary and Ill at Ease* (Leominster: Gracewing, 1993), p. 180.

16 Rees, *Weary and Ill at Ease* pp. 100–5.

17 There is a debate over whether Paul authored Ephesians, although even some who are unconvinced of his authorship are willing to describe the epistle as "Pauline" (e.g. John S. Spong, *Re-Claiming the Bible for a Non-Religious World* (New York: HarperCollins, 2013), p. 289).

18 Mary McGann, *Exploring Music as Worship and Theology* (Collegeville, MN: Liturgical Press, 2002), p. 71. © 2002 by Order of Saint Benedict, Collegeville, MN. Used with permission.

19   See, for example, *In Tune with Heaven,* pp. 48–9; Veli-Matti Karkkainen, *Pneumatology* (Grand Rapids, MI: Baker Academic, 2002), pp. 91–2.

20   See, for instance, Arnold, *Sacred Music in Secular Society,* (Farnham: Ashgate, 2014), p. 118, 146.

21   See Gordon Fee, *Paul, the Spirit, and the People of God* (Grand Rapids, MI: Baker Academic, 2011), pp. 106ff; 124.

22   Rowan Williams, "The Holy Spirit in the Bible", in Jane Williams (ed.), *The Holy Spirit in the World Today* (London: Alpha, 2011), p. 65. See also Graham Tomlin, "Life in the Spirit", in Jane Williams (ed.), *The Holy Spirit in the World Today* (London: Alpha, 2011), p. 83.

23   Williams, "The Holy Spirit in the Bible", p. 70.

24   Steven Guthrie, "The Wisdom of Song", in Jeremy Begbie and Steven Guthrie (eds), *Resonant Witness* (Grand Rapids, MI: Eerdmans, 2011), pp. 398–403.

25   This is suggested by the way the behaviour described by Guthrie reflects the "fruit of the Spirit" as outlined by Paul in Galatians 5:22–23: "But the fruit of the Spirit is love, joy, peace, forbearance, kindness, goodness, faithfulness, gentleness and self-control." For a useful fleshing out of what each fruit means, see Fee, *Paul, the Spirit, and the People of God,* pp. 116–23.

26   Quoted in Lucy Winkett, *Our Sound is our Wound* (London: Continuum, 2010), p. 77.

27   Guthrie, "The Wisdom of Song", p. 401.

28   Guthrie, "The Wisdom of Song", p. 402, his italics. Begbie points out how music is naturally inclusive in that a single note can fill my "aural space", yet there is still room for harmonizing notes: " . . . an uncrowded, expansive space without clear edges, where

distinct voices mutually establish and enhance one another." (Jeremy Begbie, *Resounding Truth* (Grand Rapids: Baker Academic, 2007), pp. 286–90.)

29 See also Begbie, *Resounding Truth,* pp. 248–50; and Thomas H. Troeger, *Music as Prayer* (Oxford: Oxford University Press, 2013), "The human creature who comes to terms with finitude is the one who lives most fully and most freely." (p. 34).

30 Karkkainen, *Pneumatology,* p. 92.

31 Guthrie, "The Wisdom of Song", p. 399.

32 Guthrie, "The Wisdom of Song", p. 399.

33 McGann, *Exploring Music as Worship and Theology,* p. 72.

34 Stacy Horn, *Imperfect Harmony* (Chapel Hill, NC: Algonquin, 2013), p. 172.

35 See Lee, *Paul, the Stoics, and the Body of Christ,* pp. 148–50. As Lee points out, Paul's likening of the body of Christ to a human body is strikingly reminiscent of the Stoic philosopher Epictetus, who also considered membership of a body to be an essential component of identity: "Do you not know that the foot, if detached, will no longer be a foot, so you too, if detached will no longer be a human being?" (Quoted on p. 141.) Lee's overall thesis, throughout her book, is that the Stoics enable us to understand in more depth Paul's concept of the body of Christ. (See also Begbie, *Resounding Truth,* pp. 269–70.)

36 As Paul puts it: "But in fact God has placed the parts in the body, every one of them, just as he wanted them to be. If they were all one part, where would the body be?" (1 Corinthians 12:18–19).

37 McGann, *Exploring Music as Worship and Theology,* pp. 70–1.

38 Erik Routley, *Church Music and the Christian Faith* (Chicago, IL: Agape, 1978), pp. 15–20, 85.

[39] See Matthew 5:41: "If anyone forces you to go one mile, go with them two miles."

[40] Fee, *Paul, the Spirit, and the People of God*, pp. 100ff.

[41] Jeremy Begbie, "Faithful Feelings", in Jeremy Begbie and Steven Guthrie, *Resonant Witness* (Grand Rapids, MI: Eerdmans, 2011), pp. 349ff.

[42] For instance, Begbie argues that, in the last movement of his "Pathétique" Symphony, Tchaikovsky differentiates "reflective grief from despairing grief". ("Faithful Feelings", p. 350.)

[43] Arnold, *Sacred Music in Secular Society*, p. 10.

[44] As an example of a group being "emotionally represented" by music, Begbie describes the funeral of a young mother who had committed suicide. At the graveside, her only son played a lament on bagpipes. Begbie's friend, who led the service, remarked that it was as if the son summed up for everyone "what we really wanted to say, deep down". ("Faithful Feelings", p. 350.)

[45] See Gooder, *Body*, p. 121.

[46] Lucy Winkett reflects the same concern in relation to the broadcast of Choral Evensong which, relaying the comment of an academic musicologist, she describes as "[having] done for church music what Barbie [has] done for women: that is, offer a perfected standard that ordinary people find hard to emulate, inducing guilt and anxiety when they can't." (*Our Sound is Our Wound*, p. 30).

[47] Quoted in Heidi Epstein, *Melting the Venusberg: A Feminist Theology of Music* (New York: Continuum, 2004), p. 123.

[48] Being distracted by the music itself was a concern shared by Augustine: "When it happens to me that the music moves me

more than the subject of the song, I confess myself to commit a sin deserving punishment, and then I would prefer not to hear the singer." (Quoted in Winkett, *Our Sound is Our Wound*, p. 79.) (See also Thomas Day, *Why Catholics Can't Sing* (New York: Crossroad, 2002), pp. 54–5.)

49 Begbie traces a longstanding tendency, by artists of various sorts (including painters, composers, philosophers and theologians) to shun the physicality of music in favour of its ability to express spiritual and intellectual ideas (*Resounding Truth*, pp. 213–19). His corrective is to suggest that "we might do well to regain a sense of music's profound physicality—its embeddedness in God's given material world." (*Resounding Truth*, p. 217.) I would urge this to include not just human bodies, but also the personalities that inhabit them.

50 Gareth Malone, *Choir* (London: Collins, 2013), p. 110.

51 Malone, *Choir,* pp. 120–1.

52 The following is based on Nicholas Taylor, *Paul on Baptism* (London: SCM, 2016), Chapter 2 and also his summary of Paul's understanding of baptism on p. 162: "What is clear from Paul's explicit statements is that in Baptism the Church receives into the fellowship of Christ's body new members, confers a Christian identity upon them, and indeed a new life free of the power of evil. In the name of God the Church invokes on those baptized the Holy Spirit to guide and empower them in their Christian lives."

53 Exactly what Paul considered that connection to be is the subject of debate. For example, Taylor considers the Spirit to be the agency of baptism—that which someone is baptized *with*—whereas Fee understands the Spirit as the substance

that someone is baptized *in* (see Taylor, *Paul on Baptism*, p. 47 footnote 37; Fee, *The First Epistle to the Corinthians*, pp. 605–6).

54 Joining a church choir is such a good introduction to Christianity that some are even creating church plants by starting choirs (see Madeleine Davies, "From the Choir Stalls to the Altar", *Church Times,* 17 November 2017).

55 Wayne Meeks describes conversion for the Pauline Christians as "an extraordinarily thoroughgoing resocialisation, in which the sect was intended to become virtually the primary group for its members, supplanting all other loyalties" (Wayne Meeks, *The First Urban Christians* (New Haven: Yale University Press, 2003), p. 78). This might be a little stronger than one's newfound loyalties to a fledgling church choir, but if conversion is even partly a matter of resocialization, one can see how membership of this micro-community would provide useful support.

56 Quoted in Arnold, *Sacred Music in Secular Society*, p. 58.

57 Erik Varden, "Translator's Preface" to Elisabeth-Paule Labat, *The Song That I Am* (Collegeville, MN: Liturgical Press, 2014), pp. xv–xvii.

58 Varden, "Translator's Preface", p. xv.

59 The way music is able to do this is reminiscent of John V. Taylor's suggestion that the Spirit is able to "open eyes" in a way that produces "double exposure by which what is and what might be are seen together in a single vision"; in a flash of inspiration (*The Go Between God* (London: SCM, 1989), p. 74).

60 Varden, "Translator's Preface", p. xv. Other examples include Arnold: "We perform music because it takes us beyond both words and reason" (*Sacred Music in Secular Society*, p. 80); Begbie: "Music is fundamentally about making and receiving

sounds, and this book is designed to show some of the theological fruit which can emerge from examining carefully what is involved in this making and reception" (Jeremy Begbie, *Theology, Music and Time* (Cambridge: Cambridge University Press, 2004), p. 5); and Saliers " . . . music offers the possibility of a way of understanding something that language may express but not fully contain" (Don E. Saliers, *Music and Theology* (Nashville, TN: Abingdon Press, 2007), p. 75).

[61] Winkett, *Our Sound is our Wound*, pp. 23–4. In a similar vein, Arnold argues for a definition of "sacred" music as that which "appeals to those needs, desires and doubts that are experienced by all thinking and truly human individuals" (*Sacred Music in Secular Society*, p. 10). Exactly what he means by this isn't clear, but the definition appears broad enough to encompass music that would not normally be associated with Christianity or indeed any religion.

[62] Wren, *Praying Twice,* pp. 9–10.

[63] "John Bercow defends plans to axe Commons clerks' wigs" (BBC News, 6 February 2017: <https://www.bbc.co.uk/news/uk-politics-38879102>).

[64] In addition to Iona and Taizé resources (see Chapter 1), the RSCM website offers some useful material to members as part of its *Lift up your Voice* course: <https://www.rscmshop.com/features/lift-up-your-voice>.

[65] Even here there are examples of communities seeking to widen participation in other ways, such as when local primary school children were invited to sing alongside experienced choristers from St Catherine's College, Cambridge, for an Ash Wednesday service on 26 February 2020. See <https://www.elydiocese.org/

about/news-jobs-and-events/news/primary-school-children-sing-alongside-world-class-choristers.php>.

66 There are many examples, including the Choir of the Nation, organized by St Paul's Cathedral in London; Gareth Malone's Great British Home Chorus; and Adam Grannick's Socially Distant Orchestra.

67 A UK Government scheme aimed at preventing mass redundancies, whereby the Government pays up to 80 per cent of an employee's salary, enabling employers to keep them on the payroll even though they are unable to work.

68 <https://www.youtube.com/watch?v=C9GYiVqqZYI>.

EU GPSR Authorized Representative:

LOGOS EUROPE, 9 rue Nicolas Poussin, 17000 La Rochelle, France

contact@logoseurope.eu

www.ingramcontent.com/pod-product-compliance
Lightning Source LLC
Chambersburg PA
CBHW070333090426
42733CB00012B/2469